BEING RUTH

BEING
RUTH

―― Being Believers ――

BEING RUTH

The Beauty in Being Godly

Rev. Archie Murray

BEING RUTH
Copyright © 2020 by Rev. Archie Murray

All rights reserved. Neither this publication nor any part of this publication may be reproduced or transmitted in any form or by any means, electronic or mechanical, including photocopying, recording or any information storage and retrieval system, without permission in writing from the author.

Unless otherwise indicated, all Scripture quotations are taken from the New King James Version®. Copyright © 1982 by Thomas Nelson, Inc. Used by permission. All rights reserved. Scripture quotations marked KJV are taken from the Holy Bible, King James Version, which is in the public domain. Scripture quotations marked ESV are from The ESV® Bible (The Holy Bible, English Standard Version®). ESV® Text Edition: 2016. Copyright © 2001 by Crossway, a publishing ministry of Good News Publishers. Used by permission. All rights reserved.

Printed in Canada

Print ISBN: 978-1-4866-1709-8
eBook ISBN: 978-1-4866-1710-4

Word Alive Press
119 De Baets Street, Winnipeg, MB R2J 3R9
www.wordalivepress.ca

WORD ALIVE
—PRESS—

FSC MIX
Paper from responsible sources
FSC® C103567

Cataloguing in Publication may be obtained through Library and Archives Canada

The Being Believers series is dedicated to my brother
Robert F. Murray

Robert led me to Jesus Christ and won me for Him when we were both teenagers. He has been a lifetime example for me, as my brother John has also been, who since early childhood made me proud.

—Rev. Archie Murray, BD, DipMin, DPT

CONTENTS

SECTION I: THE GODLY, BEING IN TROUBLE

1. Being Tragic Times — 3
2. Migration to Misery — 5
3. Who Is the Story About? — 9
4. Being Well-Named With a Pleasant Wife — 11
5. Being the Meaning of Your Name — 15
6. A Good Address — 19
7. Being Bereaved — 21
8. Being Foreign Wives — 25
9. The Beauty in Being Godly — 29
10. Too Much Death — 31

SECTION II: CHANGE BEING IN THE AIR

11. Grief Being Observed — 35
12. Being an Exhortation from the 4th Century — 37
13. Being Like the Prodigal — 39
14. Being Repentant — 43
15. Being Too Focused — 47

SECTION III: BEING BROKEN TALK

16. The Godly Giving Bad Advice — 53

SECTION IV: TEARS

17. Weeping Being Weak — 59
18. Words Being Weak — 63
19. A Sound Case Being Wrong — 67

SECTION V: BEING SPEECHES

20.	Orpah Being Orpah	73
21.	Naomi Failing to Be Naomi	77
22.	Ruth Becoming Ruth	81.
23.	Divine Words in a Woman's Voice	83

SECTION VI: RUTH SPEAKS; GOD SPEAKS

24.	The Entreaty	87
25.	Being Committed to Love	89
26.	Do Not Urge Me to Leave You	91
27.	Or to Return from Following You	95
28.	Where You Go I Will Go	97
29.	Where You Lodge I Will Lodge	101
30.	Your People Shall Be My People	103
31.	And Your God My God	107
32.	Where You Die I Will Die	111
33.	And There Will I Be Buried	113
34.	The Lord Do So to Me and More Also If Anything But Death Parts Me from You	115
35.	The Silent Walk	117

SECTION VII: GOD KNOWS YOUR NAME

36.	God Knows Your Name	123
37.	Being Stuck	127
38.	The Godless Algorithm	131

SECTION VIII: BARLEY HARVEST

39.	A New Beginning	137
40.	A Rich Relative	141
41.	The Moabite Becomes My Daughter	143
42.	Gleaning	147

SECTION IX: BEING EXAMINED

43.	Whose Young Woman Is This?	153
44.	Being a Listener	157
45.	Being Focused	163
46.	Being Young Men	165
47.	Being Grateful	167
48.	Being Comforted	171

SECTION X: BEING PROVIDED FOR

49.	Gleaning Among the Sheaves	177
50.	The Discovery	181

SECTION XI: NAOMI IS BACK

51.	Being Partners	187
52.	Naomi Is Back!	191
53.	Being Prepared	193
54.	Then and Only Then	199

SECTION XII: THE THRESHING FLOOR

55.	Going Down	207
56.	Being an Ambassador	211
57.	Being Exhausted	213

SECTION XIII: A STRANGE QUIET WORLD

58.	Being Quiet	217
59.	Being at Midnight	219
60.	Who Are You?	223
61.	My Daughter	225
62.	My Town	231
63.	Being Willing to Let Go	235
64.	Being Discrete	241
65.	The Garment	245

SECTION XIV: BEING BOAZ

66.	Being Weighed Down with Blessing	251
67.	Waiting	253
68.	Being a Finisher	257

SECTION XV: IN THE GATE

69.	The Fulcrum	263
70.	Being Unable	267
71.	Being Tenants	273
72.	Being Witnesses	279
73.	The Widow Becomes a Wife	283
74.	The Place of Influence	287
75.	Being Bobby Hamilton	291

SECTION XVI: GOD'S PURPOSE BEING FULFILLED

76.	Being Superstars	299
77.	Being the Descendants of Boaz and Ruth	301
78.	The Lord Gives Conception	305
79.	Obed Being the Father of Jesse, Being the Father of David	309
80.	God's Purpose Being a Wee Boy	311

About the Author	313

ACKNOWLEDGEMENTS

Writing this book has been a great joy. Many people were excited that I had chosen to write on the book of Ruth, because it is such a highly loved Bible book. I cannot possibly do it justice, but I have done what I could.

I want to thank two churches for helping me to teach God's Word. My first pastorate was in Orangefield Baptist Church in Greenock, Scotland, for twelve years. Particularly the youth group, the worship team, and some choice friends showed me what it is to walk with God.

I also thank First Lobo Baptist Church in Ontario, Canada, for my thirteen years of ministry and particularly Bruce and Betsy Lively, the deacons, the worship team, and the youth group. I am most grateful for my final year at Lobo, the most satisfying year of my entire pastoral ministry. During both of those pastorates I wrote a lot for my congregation. In the last few years of ministry I felt a desire to give myself more fully to writing. This is my second book as a result of that decision. My third in this series, *Being Joshua*, is now being written.

The publisher, Word Alive Press, Sylvia St Cyr, Katelyn Boulanger, Lori Mackay, and the team there have been superb throughout the last few years. I have learned so much and been helped in the publishing process immensely. With Word Alive I have had the sense of being supported by friends.

No books would ever have been written without the constant prayerful, patient support of my wife, Helen. Thank you to my daughter Rosslyn, for her companionship in writing this book and for her beautiful life. To my daughter Allison, for her energetic encouragement and love. To my son, Jonathan, who helped me become a man. And in this context, I thank my son Michael and his wife, Martha, particularly for their persistent exhortations to me to write as many books as I can over the next ten years for their children, Emmett, Brooklyn, and Victoria, our grandchildren.

There are also unnamed individuals who have given me encouragement, support, and love over many long years for whom I thank God daily.

I commend this little book, about the little book of Ruth, to you, and I pray that the Lord will make it a blessing.

Archie

(Rev. Archie Murray, BD, DipMin, DPT)

INTRODUCTION

The book of Ruth—it's just a wee book. It has four chapters and is about five pages long in my Bible. How is it that such a tiny work has lasted so many centuries and still holds a high place in the hearts of so many readers? To claim it is "inspired by God" may be strange to the man of the world, but centuries of readers have declared this with consistent confidence. Divine inspiration has been the only explanation for the amazing longevity of the beautiful book of Ruth. Ruth displays the beauty in being godly.

The book has a forlorn atmosphere from the very beginning. Very soon you find your brow down, your breath shortened or deepened, subconsciously monitoring your concentration. The narrative captures you. It is brief, concise. Almost musical, almost staccato, but the movement is as though it were legato!

A characteristic of all the books in the biblical canon is that there is no wastage of words. The book of Ruth flows; it does not rush. Simple yet substantial, it's a short story, but it has outlived cultures and centuries and remains with us today and is still loved today.

The eternal plan of God for our salvation is revealed in these few short pages, veiled and soft, vibrant and powerful. The message is how God brings together the seemingly haphazard circumstances of life. He then weaves them into a perfect series of events. These events run from before time began, before the world and men were created, all the way through time itself and into eternity forever.

Sometimes we think eternity stopped during the period we call time; then it will start up again when time ends. But eternity has no stop. It had no start! It is not continual as such; it is more of a

Being Ruth

constant. Eternity is like this idea of "being"—it is something that is. It does not fluctuate, does not come and go; it is always. It is without the thing we call "time." However, the message of the Bible is one that had its origins in eternity; for us it is fundamentally outworked in time, and we will find its fruition in eternity. This is a workable way for us to look at it.

Watercolour paint is a gentle medium. However, it can be strong, as seen, for example, in the work of the 18th century artist John Constable. His painting entitled *Stonehenge*, "widely regarded as one of the greatest watercolors ever," is filled with "bold contrasts of light and dark…you feel that mixture of inspiration and foreboding."[1] The book of Ruth is like such a watercolour painting. The narrative softly unwraps the gentle lives of two godly women. At the same time it lays upon them bold divine themes like godliness, redemption and providence. It takes the bright and hopeful aspects of life like love, marriage, and family, and sits them firmly in the darkness of death and desertion. All the contrasts enhance one another. Here in the book of Ruth, we have the divine mission laid out. Rich in contrasts, and certainly at times filled with foreboding, yet the book's overall impression remains warm, soft, and appealing to the believing heart, because life's contrasts, even life's contradictions, reveal in the believer a beauty in being godly.

As in most spiritual moments, God's divine plan, His divine provision, though always there is only recognized by those who take the time to look. Even unbelievers can see God's hand declared throughout the pages of the Bible. That is, if they read with an open mind. They can see it to a sufficient degree to recognize the message but are unable to appropriate it to themselves. That is, until the Holy Spirit draws them and they seek the Lord, and God opens their hearts. Until then, unbelievers remain, at best, educated but in unbelief.

---

1 Christopher Muscato, "Comparing Watercolor, Aquatint, and Oil Paint During the Romantic Period," Study.com, https://study.com/academy/lesson/comparing-watercolor-aquatint-oil-paint-during-the-romantic-period.html.

The message of the book of Ruth is magnificent and essentially significant to the plan of God. The message is that God is working out His divine purposes in and through the lives of ordinary men and women. In the book of Ruth it is two godly women who shine. They are both particularly beautiful people. Both are deep and humble. Both are servants of God, of the highest calibre.

For the most part the book remains firmly on the ground and embedded in daily lives. At the end it does rise and show its events to be a divine intervention in the affairs of men, furthering God's plan of salvation through His Son, the Lord Jesus Christ. the book is rich with lessons for life and reveals clearly how beautiful it is to be godly.

There is a humbling that settles on the reader. Perhaps it is caused by the instant sadness of the narrative. Sadness, whatever the cause, is like a picture frame. It sets us into the confines of our human frailty. Strangely, the reader in the early stages of the book is not merely an observer. As the initial compounding tragedies unfold, the Bible makes us an integral part of events. Yet, while being drawn into this story, we still feel restrained. It feels as if the events know we are watching, know we are close, yet refuse our comment or interjection. It might be described as thought provoking.

Initially, it simply puts us into a sad suspension. We may watch but keep our distance; there is too much pain to be shared. If we let the narrative captivate our minds, it will quickly penetrate our hearts.

The story holds the readers still, not motionless, because God is working! He is working something into the heart of the readers as they read! *"For whatever things were written before were written for our learning, that we through the patience and comfort of the Scriptures might have hope"* (Romans 15:4).

The book of Ruth begins with a journey. The family moves from Israel to the country of Moab. There, the family is decimated! Yet out of the darkness hope remains through all of its shades, until faith is fully justified. It is a journey born out of human desperation, not out of any call or promise from God. There is no mention of God in the decision to take the journey to Moab. It is simply seen as the solution to famine. Often genuine decisions of our own, intended to take us out of famine, just result in a different sort of famine sooner or later.

The lessons we observe here in this little book apply to all kinds of famine. Any kind of human pain caused by a lack of something can be described as a famine. These situations may or may not be caused by sin or disobedience. They fit just as naturally in the godly life as they do in the disobedient or rebellious. In the ungodly, they are often, but not always, brought to punish. In the godly life they can display God's grace as seen in humble acceptance of God's will. Indeed, acceptance with thanksgiving and praise! Being godly is being thankful whatever He sends our way. That thankfulness in want is a beauty with substance.

God often does what we do not understand. He allows what we would not allow, uses what we would not use—uses people we would not use! A bit like a certain Samaritan in a story told by Jesus, no less! The time-honoured title of the story is "The 'Good' Samaritan," indicating that he was a challenge to the common perception!

The character of the book of Ruth does not seem to be judgmental. The story exposes moments that can be seen as failures in a few of the participants; however, nobody is raised to be condemned. Ruth's character is the character of this book—a beautiful, godly character. But still the story spatters Ruth and the reader with trouble in the early stages.

Despite the almost total demise of this family in the first few verses, the story remains throughout encapsulated in that same divine institution, the family. The book of Ruth begins with a desperately troubled family. It ends with a glorious genealogy, the family line of the Messiah. They did not know His name, but we do—His name is Jesus!

SECTION I:
THE GODLY, BEING IN TROUBLE

chapter one

BEING TRAGIC TIMES

The Judges

Now it came to pass, in the days when the judges ruled, that there was a famine in the land. And a certain man of Bethlehem, Judah, went to dwell in the country of Moab, he and his wife and his two sons.

—Ruth 1:1

"*In the days when the judges ruled*": this phrase puts the story in a historical time frame. The setting is between the time of Joshua and Samuel. A time of vacillation between faithfulness and apostasy among the people of God—apostasy followed consequently by the oppression of Israel's enemies. They were finally to be delivered by men raised up by God called the judges. These judges guided Israel back to the Lord. After a period of faithfulness God delivered them from their enemies.

So the cycle went on. This period of Israel's history has been called a "tragic state of affairs."[2] To read, then, that the nation of Israel was in a famine at this time raises the thought that there may be a connection between judges ruling and famine. The population often blames the rulers for trouble. This is too convenient an explanation, too comfortably remote from the individual! Trouble is seldom from a distant source. Problems are much more commonplace, more often at our own door.

---

2 Edward J. Young, *An Introduction to the Old Testament,* rev. ed. (Grand Rapids, Michigan: William B. Eerdmans, 1964), 170.

God says to Cain when he is upset that the Lord rejected his offering, "*If you do not do well, sin lies at the door*" (Genesis 4:7). The problem is generally in the heart and home of the individual. The Bible teaches that the cause of many problems in the world is in fact the state of the Church in its individual members. "*If My people who are called by My name will humble themselves, and pray and seek My face, and turn from their wicked ways, then I will hear from heaven, and will forgive their sin and heal their land*" (2 Chronicles 7:14). The Bible also presents a counterbalance to the extreme idea that every kind of trouble is a result of personal failure. God calls Job "*a blameless and upright man, one who fears God and shuns evil*" (Job 1:8). Yet Job endured much suffering.

chapter two

MIGRATION TO MISERY

The family in the book of Ruth is in straits similar to many today who likewise are escaping famine to find a future. This family does find a new country, a new home, and they find that hope of a better future—initially!

However, within a short time their migration turned to misery. The curse of Eden tumbles down through the history of mankind, and the cold spectre of death suddenly shocks and chills this migrant family. And death it is of a particularly bitter sort: the death of loved ones, and multiple deaths—an exponential agony. They leave Bethlehem to flee a famine of food, only to discover a famine of family! How is it that, out of such grave ground, beauty can blossom? Ruth appears and perfumes the ugliness of human experience with the beauty of being godly. Such is the story of Ruth in its early moments.

The initial sense of futility the story conveys is felt by many today who thought they had found a promised land in the Western world. Because of war or persecution or just circumstances beyond their control, they had to leave behind countless treasures—a family, a home, little keepsakes, a mountain or a river, a valley. Perhaps more so, a birthplace, the gravestone of a loved one, a life-changing moment. Perhaps it was just an atmosphere, the air they breathed, the smells they smelled, the forgotten memories those sensations revived in an instant. And nothing in this land of promise has been able to replace them. Quietly the fears and torments of the old country can be replaced by a fearful sense of floating in unfamiliar air. Nothing feels solid; there's no comfort from the familiar and certainly no ownership of anything substantial.

Being Ruth

Many aspects of life could be expressed by the word *family*. The hope is to revisit and experience them when the traveller returns to visit home. While home is always home, only few memories remain untainted, so that in fact they may have to reluctantly admit to themselves that "home" is no longer. The memories all seem so far away, and few seem to wait for them, at least as they were.

When an immigrant returns to what we called "home," it can be jarringly different from what we remember. It is difficult to tell whether it is just the impression on our minds made by the newness or novelty of our new home or whether the original home has actually changed since we left. Probably it is a mix of both. The new home may never provide that emotion, that priceless feeling, enshrined in the word *home*. This writer is no longer a Scot. Nor, despite fifteen years and citizenship, a Canadian. It takes the two to construct one half-hearted sense of belonging, a "Scots Canadian"—what is that when the heart longs for "home"?

There is a hint of a similar sense of broken belonging in Paul's cry for the salvation of his own people, the Jews: *"For I could wish that I myself were accursed from Christ for my brethren, my countrymen according to the flesh"* (Romans 9:3). He was persecuted to the point of death by them. He has been travelling away from home for a long time. Yet there remained deep inside him a longing for a better memory of home. A longing for their salvation. Surely this is, in part, a prayer for healing in his own memory of his people, his home. A memory tinged with pain unhealed. This was due to their ongoing rejection of himself but also, and more so, their continued rejection of their Messiah. Home in all its aspects should be a good memory.

So we have an intensely miserable start to the story. Yet we do not stop reading! Those who begin to read the book of Ruth are compelled to keep reading and, indeed, to read with a deeper mind. Why? Is it because there is something placed within the human heart that desperately has to find a good ending to tragedy? To find order in chaos? We keep reading hoping for change, for improvement. We need a rational that will ease our mind as we watch innocents suffer, even though human innocence is a doubtful concept. We search for a purpose for seemingly pointless pain. Even the atheist wants some answers. When no answer is evident, he blames the God he does not believe exists. He must do this because only God can give hope when there is none.

We look for that light at the end of the tunnel. The book of Ruth gives us such a light. It brings us in a few short pages to the glorious light of the world, Jesus Christ. He is God's answer. The Messiah was already, by Ruth's day, an old prophetic hope. There was still a long time to come before it would be fulfilled. It would be fulfilled, but not without Ruth!

chapter three

WHO IS THE STORY ABOUT?

The name of the man was Elimelech, the name of his wife was Naomi, and the names of his two sons were Mahlon and Chilion—Ephrathites of Bethlehem, Judah.

—Ruth 1:2

Names

Who is this story about? One thing becomes clear quickly: it is not about the *"certain man."* Nevertheless, he is where the story begins. Ruth 1:1 says, *"A certain man of Bethlehem, Judah, went to dwell in the country of Moab."* This introduction to the story is not insignificant. It is, interestingly, a little misleading. It sets us up to expect something significant about this "certain man."

He was of Bethlehem, Judah, part of the nation of God's people. However, the certain man himself is not the significant person in the story. It is his wife, Naomi, who will be the star initially; then she is joined by Ruth. Of course Ruth is who the book is really about. However, note that the Scriptures gives this man a name, telling us that whether you are important or insignificant, God knows your name!

Let's just think about these names before we get in to the story proper. They are there for a purpose. They are interesting. The names of these biblical characters are normal names for the time and culture in Israel, or Moab. There is regularly a meaning behind their name that has significance for events in their lives or times. The meaning can even be a prophetic suggestion for the future of their lives or for others. If we have to use too much imagination to find some significance in a name, we probably should ignore it for the time being. But these names are clearly significant.

Also, and particularly at the time of this story, there is a comment on the men of the time. At the very end of the book of Judges, a description of "everyone" is given to us. It says, *"Everyone did that which was right in his own eyes"* (Judges 21:25). This description supersedes any description found in a man's birth name. It is negative! it suggests that even what they thought was right may not have been right! Israel was supposed to do what God told them to do. The comment is a significant and sad truth at this time when there was *"no king in Israel"* (Judges 21:25). God was meant to be the King of Israel.

chapter four

BEING WELL-NAMED WITH A PLEASANT WIFE

Elimelech Means "My God Is King"

This is the name of that *"certain man"* who starts the book of Ruth. What can we make of this wonderful name "my God is King"? Does this name indicate for us something about Elimelech?

The tendency upon reading the story is to write him off as a failure. He took his family out of Bethlehem, Judah, landed them in a heathen culture, and left them widowed and fatherless. Well, yes, he did! But Elimelech did not plan his own early demise! He may have been a caring husband and father. His only wish was to feed his children. Did some of those who stayed in Bethlehem, Judah, also die, or even see their children die, in the famine? We don't know! The trouble is just that—we do not know enough, yet we often set Elimelech apart for special censure. This is quite understandable and may indeed be justifiable. But we can have a tendency to judge others too harshly.

Matthew Henry is never too harsh. Actually, his is one of the most loved Bible commentaries of all time, partly because it is a devotional commentary, as opposed to a theological commentary. However, he gives Elimelech no excuse for leaving Bethlehem, Judah. While he commends him for his care for his family, he will not accept that the circumstances called for his departure from the people of God. Others survived the famine with less than Elimelech had. But Henry suggests that Elimelech perhaps was not willing to accept this restraint, even though he had a small family by comparison to many others who remained in Bethlehem.[3] The fact that Naomi had to return to Bethlehem, Judah, might also be seen as a final case against Elimelech.

His name however, might just caution us from making too much of one man's failure. His awesome name may be intended to balance any careless rejection we feel. There may be a case to suggest that the godly comment contained in his name tells us that Elimelech was indeed a man who still held the conviction that "my God is King." A moment of desperation, a chance opportunity to save his family—any number of circumstances could have arisen that we ourselves would have jumped at to get away from famine.

However, it is more likely that the name reminds us that even when we do run away from God, even when we do that which is right in our own eyes but not in His, still "my God is King"! Elimelech's name reminds us that even when there is no visible outward authority, no "king" for the believer, the godly man, God is still our King and must be obeyed.

We must remember that his decision was used by this God who was his King to further His own grand design. Ruth the Moabitess was planned by God long before Elimelech left Bethlehem, Judah. Elimelech may well have had attitudes and responses to the Holy Spirit's leading that we will never know about in this life, especially in light of the brief mention he gets in the narrative. We are also too far away from the matter, and the man, to be able to judge too confidently.

We should not be surprised when in eternity we are given fascinating insights about those characters in the biblical record who receive little detailed attention. Many of them may be heroes in heaven. Here on this earth, in this story, Elimelech's part in the providence of God is to mistakenly take his family to Moab, there to die. Do not be surprised if he then went to his reward in heaven. It is not, in the final analysis, our place to determine another man's decisions in a famine! He is, after all, given the most significant

---

3 Matthew Henry, *Matthew Henry's Commentary on the Whole Bible*, vol. 1 (n.p.: Hendrickson Publishers, 1991), 198.

name in his family. Like most of the names, they are hiding in translation, for us to find and ponder about.

"My God is King"—here in this name is a statement of submission to the entire will of God. A statement that is satisfied with whatever the Lord asks or sends and is willing to obey, no matter the consequences. Many will think this is too much to even ponder on silence. But his name may be there to break the silence! One thing we can gain encouragement from is that God can turn our mistakes to serve His purposes, because "my God is King"!

Naomi Means "My Amiable or Pleasant One"

Naomi, Elimelech's wife, tells us this is the meaning of her name when she returns home destitute. She says, *"Do not call me Naomi [pleasant]; call me Mara [bitter]"* (Ruth 1:20). Yet she was well named "Pleasant," was she not? Is the woman we read of in the story not amiable and pleasant?

Yes, she certainly is. Indeed it could be argued that Naomi stands equal in stature to Ruth throughout the book called "Ruth." Hear her appeal to her daughters-in-law (Ruth 1:8-9). Is this not, on the surface at least, gentle and pleasant? That, despite the fact that her early circumstances were anything but "pleasant." This description of her will shine again once she is back home in Bethlehem, Judah.

So we see clearly that to Naomi's society and culture, names and their meaning were important in a way we no longer regard them. Naomi's appeal to the people upon her return to her home is an argument based upon the meaning of her name.

Elimelech and Naomi have beautiful names. Their reason therefore for giving their two sons such cruel names must raise interest. Were they based on some knowledge that is not shared here in the story? A difficult pregnancy, a difficult birth—twice? One wonders what gave rise to these incredibly depressing names! Could it be that for a moment Naomi and Elimelech simply followed a fashion and did not even bother to check the meaning of these names? Now that would have been a lesson for us today!

The Bible is too busy with a greater story than to satisfy our curiosity. Life is often very complicated. Trying to read the lives of others from a great distance is difficult, especially when we recognize that many of us cannot make a lot of sense out of our own lives. But we are encouraged to examine details and to search, up to a point. So what of these two names?

chapter five

BEING THE MEANING OF YOUR NAME

Mahlon Means "Sick"

What parent would name their child "Sick"? What are we to make, if anything, of this name? Well, we should state, fairly quickly, that many a child has had a name with a meaning that did not represent anything about them at all. But, as we have also noted, sometimes a name has had a quiet significance that went unnoticed. Here there are at least two obvious connections.

The first is that Mahlon, son of Naomi and Elimelech and husband of Ruth, died childless. We know that Ruth was fertile as she had a child by Boaz later in the story. So he was a man who could not—or at least did not—have children and who died young. His name perhaps describes him accurately. Could it be that his parents knew he was sick from birth with some disorder unmentioned here and so had this expectation of an unhealthy or unfruitful life in one way or another and that he probably would die young? There is seldom any prior warning in Old Testament times as to the condition of a child at birth—unless of course those ancients understood far more than we give them credit for.

Mahlon lived up to his name and died young, leaving a childless wife. Ruth had no hope of help in old age and had none of the comfort or security spoken of in this book in connection with marriage and children. One way or another, Mahlon was well named! His brother, strangely, likewise.

Being Ruth

Chilion Means "Consumption"

Matthew Henry says that the name of Chilion, son of Naomi and Elimelech and husband of Orpah, means "consumption" (a wasting disease).[4] Strange that the parents gave both boys such devastating names! Chilion also died as Mahlon did early in life—and childless! Not a good start to a story!

Yet we read on. Why? Perhaps because every one of us has some aspect of "dismal" in our own lives. This very misery is often what unites us as humanity. Our sufferings do certainly unite us more than our pleasures do. We feel an empathy for Naomi at the loss of her husband and two young sons. Her experience reminds us of our own losses, and we sense a fellowship in suffering as we enter the narrative of the book of Ruth.

Things may appear pointless when we are looking at them through our distorted human vision, a vision damaged by the fall in Eden, like every other faculty known to us. But note this: out of all this sickness and death God will bring Ruth! She will shine like the sun though history and keep this family in the hearts and minds of God's people, to this day!

More wonderful, more awesome, is that in the story of Ruth all the characters are engaged in bringing the reader to the incarnation of God's dear Son, the Lord Jesus Christ—still a great way off for them, but for us the plan of God in sending His Son is an event almost complete in time. We are the Church on the edge of eternity; without doubt we are in the end days of this world. Our weary creation groans for its own redemption.

Jesus predicted it: *"And there will be famines, pestilences, and earthquakes in various places"* (Matthew 24:6–7). Paul felt this agony when he said, *"For we know that the whole creation groans and labors with birth pangs together until now"* (Romans 8:22). Surely the diverse earthquakes and tsunamis and volcanic ruptures in nature we are reading about in the news today are evidence of this groaning?

---

4 Henry, *Commentary on the Whole Bible*, 198.

Being the Meaning of Your Name

Strangely, in this great story of redemption, Mahlon and Chilion came so close as to have a mention. These two names sum up the whole of the human race. We are sick and wasting and in dire need of redemption. God will provide an answer in His Son, and this story tells us how this little episode was outworked.

chapter six

A GOOD ADDRESS

The family members were Ephrathites of Bethlehem, Judah. That's a good address!

Ephrathites

Ephratha means "fruitfulness." It is the ancient name of Bethlehem or a region around Bethlehem, suggesting that they lived close to what was then Bethlehem proper or to distinguish which part of the neighbourhood of Bethlehem they came from. In Jacob's time it was called Ephrath, and it was the place where Rachel was buried. So the family members were Ephrathites.

Bethlehem

Bethlehem means "house of bread." So putting these two names into place, this was a family of Ephrathites of Bethlehem. Bethlehem was in the hill country of Judah.

Judah

Judah means "praised." It was so called after the conquest of Canaan to distinguish it from Bethlehem proper because it was close to the town of Bethlehem. Hence the full description of this family is given as *"Ephrathites of Bethlehem, Judah"* (Ruth 1:2).

So a great deal of detail is used to establish a distinguished heritage. Here this family may be being presented to us as weak physically, but they are also being shown to be worthy of great respect in Israel. Today we might say they had a good address. They certainly did in terms of the meaning of the names associated with their home. It was "fruitful," "the house of bread" and "praised"! That's a lot of good things. Yet they left it all because this blessed house of bread, for a while, had none! Blessings can be removed in the good providence of God for reasons we may never understand until eternity. However, in this story, blessings are restored later in that same good providence and for that same good purpose of our good God.

chapter seven

BEING BEREAVED

Then Elimelech, Naomi's husband, died; and she was left, and her two sons.

—Ruth 1:3

We arrive at verse 3. This is the start of the narrative detailing the things that happened to the family. They have left their home. They have tried to settle in a foreign land. Instead of a bright new beginning, the story turns dark.

We know so little about Elimelech himself! The mention of him being Naomi's husband might draw a little affection from the reader. Apart from that, Elimelech comes right at the start of the book and introduces the theme of death. That theme will continue through the opening five verses of the book of Ruth. It begins with this statement: *"Then Elimelech, Naomi's husband, died."*

Death is a defining factor about mankind. When great people die, like kings, queens, or statesmen, it can introduce the end of a culture. Death can leave in its wake interminable complications for those left behind. Even the ordinary old man or woman can leave a great blessing or a great curse. Mostly, of course, it is somewhere in the middle. Sadly, for too many, even in the Western world, it can go unnoticed. Elimelech died, and whatever anyone else may have thought or felt, we are instantly aware of a significant loss: Naomi was "left"! The emptiness caused by death is a constant symptom of the human condition. This fact hangs over every man, woman, and child. It is one fact we can predict about ourselves with absolute, heavy certainty.

Today we are not able to face difficult realities. Death separates people from the living irreversibly. They have gone to a place beyond our reach. We seem to be unwilling to sit and look at it, this thing called death. We turn away. We squirm inside. We make all sorts of excuses for not naming it and claiming it as our present reality. We cannot find rest in this place.

We call the service a "memorial of a life," but there is a coffin, often an open casket, in the room, with the lifeless body of a loved one silently, even perhaps peacefully, declaring death louder than all our wordy denials. The memorabilia of the loved one are all there, but their reminders fail to please, unless we shut out the fact that they are dead. Yet they merely ratify the fact.

Why are we so afraid to mourn the reality of death? Why do we coat it and cover it and avoid it by repeating the life in flat, lifeless pictures? In things from days that are long gone! All of which are legitimate in their proper place, but our indulgence can look like faithless denial.

Is it because we feel defeated by death and are trying to recreate the life just for a little bit longer? Jesus may well be saying to us at this moment *"Oh you of little faith"* (Matthew 8:26). The believer, while faced with loss and thoroughly sad, can still rejoice over death. The presence of death is the exact moment when we need to believe that death is not the end! We know that Jesus rose from the grave having defeated death and hell. He broke its bars and rose triumphant for us! So death for us has lost its sting, as Paul says so triumphantly: *"O Death, where is your sting? O Hades, where is your victory?"* (1 Corinthians 15:55). The Christians' message in death is not that the life gone still remains in memories or trinkets but that the life now ended decisively and actually will be raised incorruptible and eternal by the resurrection power of Jesus Christ and that we will meet again in heaven. The emphasis has quietly shifted from rejoicing in an eternal life in heaven to a concentration on the valid value of memorabilia, wrongly elevated above the heavenly hope of the Church, so that the secular funeral is only marginally different to the believer's funeral.

Being Bereaved

The believer can look death in the eye, so to speak, and defy it. So the death of a loved one offers the opportunity for a powerful Christian statement of faith, and the venue for that demonstration and declaration is the public funeral service. The world tries so hard to get the reality of death out of the service of remembrance, but the believer must keep death in it! It is the opportunity for the deceased to make a lasting testimony, to declare Christ's victory and to declare our faith and demonstrate the power of the resurrection. The funeral service is an obvious opportunity for this statement of faith to be made. This is Paul's reasoning:

> *But I do not want you to be ignorant, brethren, concerning those who have fallen asleep, lest you sorrow as others who have no hope. For if we believe that Jesus died and rose again, even so God will bring with Him those who sleep in Jesus.*
> —1 Thessalonians 4:13–14

Mortal man is unable to handle death without the truth of the resurrection of Jesus Christ. Only the believer can cope. And we must declare our strength as coming from Him and not of ourselves, to give Him the glory.

In this story Naomi is left. The Bible leaves us to imagine her grief. She is initially left with her two sons. No doubt they were a comfort to one another in their loss of a husband and a father.

Elimelech's death is not set at a specific time for us other than to establish that it was before the sons married. Elimelech probably died quite soon after they arrived in Moab. He died in a foreign country before he had time to naturalize or become a part of that society. It takes a long time to fully integrate into a foreign land. Certainly a period of years, maybe ten—maybe never! He was buried there, a long way from home. There is a deep human sadness in this state of affairs. People will transport the bodies of loved ones around the world to take them back to their roots for final burial. Often there remains an unsettling, inconclusive feeling when a person dies away from home. "Lost at sea" is often surreal for the family of such a one. These are out of the ordinary deaths. They take longer to "die." Elimelech unexpectedly dying as a relatively young man would have been a similar situation. The family would grieve longer than normal.

Only a few things are presented to us in the narrative to identify Elimelech. He has a good name. He married a good woman called Naomi. He left Bethlehem, the house of bread. He had two sons. He had an untimely death.

"And she was left, and her two sons." The book has not travelled many verses yet, so to speak, and we are left with a widow and two fatherless children as our focus! Yet we read on. What an amazing sense of hope the book of Ruth exerts. Even when presenting us with human misery it draws us on to see how God works it all out.

chapter eight

BEING FOREIGN WIVES

Now they took wives of the women of Moab: the name of the one was Orpah, and the name of the other Ruth. And they dwelt there about ten years.

—Ruth 1:4

So the introduction to this story has ended. It covered the subject of how they got to Moab and what happened there. Now we move on to the next phase, the introduction of Ruth. Where did she come from? How did she become part of this record of the Holy Scriptures? How does she—from a heathen background—become godly? How does she become such an integral part of the story of redemption? That is what we are about to observe as we read.

The two sons take wives of the women of Moab. Here we see what might be yet another human attempt at solving another human problem. Dad has gone; let's get married and raise a family and settle here in Moab. Let's make this our home! God had different intentions.

"*The women of Moab*" is a phrase worth stopping to consider. Why does the Bible tell us that they took wives of the women of Moab? Why not just say "they took wives"? Why the mention of nationality? Is it not obvious? Perhaps it is to reinforce for us the extent of their Moabite integration, to expose the fact that Ruth and Orpah are not Israelites. To take foreign wives was always seen as a bad thing in Israel. The purity of the race of Israel was of paramount importance. Foreign women had always taken God's people away from Him, to their own gods or to no god, which is in reality the same thing! Even as late, in relative historical terms, as Nehemiah's day, the people were called to forsake their foreign wives as an evidence of repentance. The New Testament equally forbids the marrying of believers with unbelievers.

Were all foreigners evil? Definitely not. Did all foreigners have "foreign gods"? Absolutely, yes, they did! Many of these nations may have been very nice, cultured, but they did not know the true God, the God of Israel. It should also be acknowledged that a significant number of these nations, including Moab, were considered then, and now, to be reprehensible in their lifestyles, even by 21st century Western standards. There can be no question that the nation of Israel stood out as a better society than many of the ancient nations in morality and development, in its laws and structure and culture. Even if at this time they had departed from the Lord and done what was right in their own eyes, they would return and again shine as a light in the darkness of ancient cultures. Israel was the people of God. They were set apart throughout the Old Testament Scriptures.

This idea of a nation set apart is also present in the New Testament. It is fundamental in the teaching of Jesus. However, in the New Testament, it is a spiritual nation. Old Testament Israel pictures this special nation, hence the view often expressed regarding Elimelech that he was guilty of deserting God's people, God's chosen race. The understanding being expressed is that he left God's nation, God's land, to go to the heathen land of Moab. Now his sons are marrying into that culture, no doubt intending to raise children in it. Children can wander far from their father's faith.

The differences between human cultures are very deep, even between those whose countries border on one another. Old cultures have history in their bones. Stop teaching history, and you will still not remove the differences. The fact is that some cultures were, and still are, better than others. They are more civilized, more educated, more just. Does this make them superior races? Well, it certainly makes them very different when compared to barbaric, uncivilized, uncaring, or violent nations.

In our world today we are afraid to note these distinctions. It cannot be helpful to be proud or arrogant and self-proclaiming. But reality speaks for itself! This family—Elimelech, Naomi and their two sons—were different from the Moabites. While they may have found food in Moab, and even wives, the culture of the God of Israel remained ingrained in them. Integration can happen, or it can be resisted effectively, according to the intentions of the individual. More often in history, mixing cultures results in their destruction, often the end of cultures—one or another or sometimes both. Most often the good in one or both cultures is corrupted by the bad in the other.

Certainly, after more than ten years in Moab Naomi is still recognizable as an Ephrathite from Bethlehem, Judah. When she returns to her homeland, she is the same person. The people ask, "*Is this Naomi?*" (Ruth 1:19), recognizing her. They name Ruth as a foreigner. But Naomi instantly blends back into the community of her old home. Despite intermarriage in her family, there appears to be no deep integration into Moabite culture evident in Naomi, even after long years in that land. Noah's "dove" only knew one safe place, the ark of God (Genesis 8:9). So Naomi will return to a safe place, her home among the people of God.

Be careful when you set out to immigrate to a foreign land. Perhaps better the devil you know than the devil you cannot even begin to imagine!

chapter nine

THE BEAUTY IN BEING GODLY

The two brothers took wives. The Bible wants to introduce us to these two young women, so it gives us their names. The first was named Orpah, meaning "neck": it indicates stubbornness.

Orpah does not play a large part in this book, though the message she proclaims is timeless. She is to be pitied because her husband died too young and left her childless. Also, because she made the wrong choice in not staying with her mother-in-law, she went into oblivion. Orpah is exposed by her name, and also in practice. She was stubborn. She would not leave her homeland. More to the point, she would not leave her gods.

The only information we are given is bad! She is given a doubtful privilege. She is named, yet she becomes a nameless signpost—silently, powerfully, telling men and women, young in particular but old as well, not to follow her example! There are many other such signposts in the Bible. The pages of history are filled with similar warnings, often bound up in or reduced to a mere name. In Orpah's case, her name would have been forgotten if not for the pages of this tiny book.

Often, names in the Bible reveal hearts more than we would like. Orpah is exposed in this little book of Ruth, a warning to any who consider going back. Here, going back to Moab is presented as failure and rejection of God. Stubbornness itself was not Orpah's problem but stubbornness coupled with unbelief—a damning mix! She went back to her gods, who are also forgotten in time.

The name of the second wife from the women of Moab was Ruth. Perhaps it means "friend." We have no certain meaning for this name. However, Ruth earned for her own name a new, fresh, and glorious meaning. It's a name with deep significance, a meaning established here in this everlasting Bible story. The original meaning, if there was one, is no longer remembered or relevant. The Ruth represented in this little book has re-created her name, defining it as "friend."

Tens of thousands have taken the name Ruth. It is a name that is loved, a gentle, kind, and gracious name. The picture we are given throughout this book is of a godly, substantial woman, showing us that those outside the fold of God's people can be brought in, can become one with us, and indeed can become examples for us. What a privilege to be able to read of Ruth and see her beauty in being godly!

chapter ten

TOO MUCH DEATH

Now they took wives of the women of Moab: the name of the one was Orpah, and the name of the other Ruth. And they dwelt there about ten years.

—Ruth 1:4

The two sons had no children in that time. Most cultures in the history of the world were, and still are, built around the family. Many today dream of the lifestyle they had, in mostly quiet rural settings, with friends and family and mutual care. In general they felt no need to travel to the ends of the earth, although some did!

Elimelech and Naomi travelled to Moab—not a very long journey; not a great distance, in terms of geography; but a great distance in terms of culture and religion! Far enough to be out of the area affected by the famine in Judah. They stayed there for ten years. That is a significant time by any reckoning, a decade, but surely it would have passed quickly for them. They were foreigners. Every day was a challenge. Every day was a novelty. Many days were difficult and trying. New discoveries, mingled with sad memories and moments, as for every foreigner in a strange land. Uncertainty, mingled with hope, spurs humans to enterprise. But here all their energetic purpose and survival instincts were to be frustrated.

It does not take much to discourage the incomer. Little things can be serious blows to their morale. Here, at the outset of this story, two husbands and a father die too young.

Being Ruth

Then both Mahlon and Chilion also died; so the woman survived her two sons and her husband.

—Ruth 1:5

This is too, too much! Too many people, too closely related. Too much tragedy. The wives are too young for such pain. Naomi is too old for such pain. They must have been devastated. They would have been the talk of the town. As we read, despite the centuries that separate us, our own hearts are moved for them.

Yet, consider this and be encouraged: they recovered! They worked through the lonely nights of the grieving process. They came through the swamp of confusion into something like a settled place. Then they try to put their lives together again. The story is still miserable, but we—we still read on!

SECTION II: CHANGE BEING IN THE AIR

chapter eleven

GRIEF BEING OBSERVED

Then she arose with her daughters-in-law that she might return from the country of Moab, for she had heard in the country of Moab that the Lord had visited His people by giving them bread.

—Ruth 1:6

Then She Arose

Naomi was effectively alone in a foreign land. So Naomi arose! Bereavement has a distinctly Christian aspect that we often forget. Our world is filled with empathetic teachings and the need to let grief have its proper time to heal. These are all good and well, even if a little idealistic. It's too easy for writers to write about grief. Grief, for the grieving, generally denies expression!

Powerful words can be reduced to no more than empty sounds, or silence, by grief. As quickly as the speed of sound, grief can atomize volumes of sound words. We think that words are all we have to offer. We have difficulty recognizing that silence is often the most eloquent option, at least initially.

Our response to death and its sense of loss is affected by our environment. The soldier on the battlefield whose best friend just died cannot stop to grieve. The grieving poor man must go to work! The grieving mother must gain control of her emotions for the sake of her children. Hopefully, in a day to come, they will be there for her. The demands of our ordinary environment often defeat our grieving. We must eat; we must sleep. Sooner, rather than later, we must work. The circumstances surrounding us affect the way we grieve. Simple ordinary things eventually demand a return to normality as best as we can express it.

Also, our belief set colours our grieving. Those for the Christian believer are the reality of God and our exercise of faith. These must affect the way we grieve. The knowledge that an all-loving and all-powerful God exists brings an overarching comfort. The Bible teaches that death itself is soon to be put away. It was defeated by the Christ on the cross. Death's only power is to jerk and twist like a dying animal, still dangerous—but defeated!

We are certain that our believing loved one has gone to heaven. What does that look like in the reality of bereavement? Surely it has a comforting influence on our sorrow. Knowing that the person who died was a believer has, for centuries, provided an unspeakable strength in bereavement. The God of the Bible is called *"the God of all comfort"* (2 Corinthians 1:3). Countless millions down through the years of time have raised their "Amens" to Paul's declaration in this text.

This world is not our home! Heaven is our home. This world, this life, is our battlefield, our struggle with sin, our opportunity to serve the Lord. Sometimes we call into question these biblical truths when we respond to leaving this world more visibly than to going to the next, which is *"far better,"* says Paul (Philippians 1:23).

The passage of time does naturally heal grief. Legitimate grief has only a relatively short life of its own. Just a few short years can gently and kindly deal with the loss of a sixty-year partnership. If grief is not fed, it too will die. Multiple deaths, as in Naomi's family, bring together the grief of a whole community. This human fellowship ministers a multiplied empathy. It serves as a counterbalance to multiplied loss. Here, the heathen and the Israelite are united in a common human experience, common in as much as death is our common lot. Naomi arose. Had she been sitting long enough, too long, in her grief? We do not know. But she arose.

chapter twelve

BEING AN EXHORTATION FROM THE 4TH CENTURY

Jerome (AD 347–420), long after Ruth but still long ago for us, wrote to a grieving woman, highlighting these very issues. Jerome is gentle with her, as with a friend, genuinely expressing empathy for her loss. Then he says, "Consider the trials which Job endured and you will see that you are over-delicate"![5] He raises the issue of her testimony, the message she is sending to the unbelieving world by her grief.

He tells her that it is reported among the neighbourhood folks that her faith in Christ has not helped her at the very time she needs help. He says that there is a danger that they will turn against the believers, like they did in another situation he mentions. Why did the heathen turn against the believers as they grieved? Because what they had been taught by this new religion they had embraced, Christianity, was hurting them. It was not helping them!

He informs the good lady in her grief that she has sent a message to the world that justifies them in what they are saying. They are reported as saying they need to get rid of these Christians, purge the city (Rome) of them, kick them into the River Tiber! Their reason? Because Christianity is not helping when they are hurting. Their new religion is not real!

Jerome also rebukes her because she is refusing to let go of a pain that she will lose naturally in the process of time anyway. So, he reasons, why hold on to something that you can't keep indefinitely?

---

5   Philip Schaff and Henry Wace, eds., *Nicene and Post-Nicene Fathers: Second Series*, vol. 6, *Jerome: Letters and Select Works* (Peabody, Massachusetts: Hendrickson Publishers, 2004), 49–54.

What's the difference? You will merely shorten what time itself will remove and see the real present benefit to your testimony! Jerome goes on at significant length to present a view of mourning that is unrecognized in the Church today, to our own selfish hurt. But much more so, to the hurt of the testimony of Christ in us if we overindulge in grieving.

Christian grief counsellors today might also gently encourage her to let it go after a reasonable time. But the reasoning would more likely be that it will harm her health. Or depress her family. We, sadly, do not see things like Jerome did, like those who made the Church great did. We can only see ourselves and our tiny little insignificant self-based culture. Our godless, shameful culture has more influence on us, at times, than the Word of God itself.

Naomi arose; what strength! This strength in Naomi is recognized by Jerome and referred to by him as an authority. Naomi is set as an example of grieving to be followed by the believers he is writing to in Rome—because she arose! Naomi arose with her daughters-in-law *"that she might return from the country of Moab"* (Ruth 1:6).

chapter thirteen
BEING LIKE THE PRODIGAL

> *Then she arose with her daughters-in-law that she might return from the country of Moab, for she had heard in the country of Moab that the LORD had visited His people by giving them bread.*
>
> —Ruth 1:6

It is interesting, but not surprising, that the heathen world talked about God's blessings to His people. The heathen in Moab talked about Bethlehem, Judah, receiving a harvest. The text says that Naomi had heard in the country of Moab that the Lord had blessed His people with bread.

God is always blessing His people with bread. Spiritual bread is the blessing we need, and only He can give it. We talk among ourselves at the end of Sunday worship or in small groups or in fellowship meetings. Sometimes for long times—an hour? Two? Does the subject of God's blessing dominate our conversation or reporting? When we meet to pray, is God's blessing a large part of our giving of thanks? If it is, it will quickly reach the ears of a world hungry for spiritual food, and they will take up the conversation. What effect will this have? It will declare to them, one and all, that the Lord lives and that He loves His people. It may have no other effect than that on the world, but somewhere among them there may be a poor backslider who will hear a call to come home. A believer who lost his or her way. A brother or sister who, for any reason, finds himself or herself having moved far away from the Lord and His people, like dear Naomi. These believers, upon hearing that God has blessed His people, just might make Naomi's decision to return, and that as a result of the heathen gossiping about the life of the Church, about God's blessings to His people. Naomi heard an attractive truth; God's people were in plenty, and she was hungry. It's the story of the prodigal, pictured for us, though Ruth and Naomi were not prodigals.

This talk of God's blessings is a good part of fellowship among God's people. Cultivate it. See the effect it had upon Naomi: the next verse says, "*Therefore she went out...to return.*"

> *Therefore she went out from the place where she was, and her two daughters-in-law with her; and they went on the way to return to the land of Judah.*
> —Ruth 1:7

This spiritual news of God's blessing in Bethlehem, Judah, had the effect of lifting these women out of mourning and into action. The action it inspired was a return to the people of God, a return to their God.

Both young women in all probability had made professions of conversion to Judaism. Both had worshipped and prayed and tithed and learned the ways of God. They had followed husbands and in-laws and become part of the people of God, though they were still in Moab. It took deep pain and the talk of good things in Israel to fill their weak spirits with enough strength to arise and go out from the place where they were. See the tremendous power in this Word! It endues God's people with power from on high. It moves churches from dead orthodoxy to living reality in relationship with God Himself and His Holy Word.

So what does this passage teach us about restoration and the returning to the Lord of those who have wandered away to whatever degree of apathy? It tells us that the local church is the source, the ground of their return. The local church in its experience of God is where the energy comes from to bring back the backsliders. Change here, at the local church, is essential; otherwise, they return to the same famine they left! Something has to change in the home church first.

When parents come home from church excited to talk about real blessing as opposed to the improvement from the new sound system or new pews—the myriad of components of the church subculture—this change to talking about real believing will lift the hopes again of a new generation. It will lift the hearts of our children and grandchildren. God's powerhouse, the focus of His energy in the world, is the local church. The church in Bethlehem, Judah, after a period of famine was being blessed! Ask the Lord to do this for your local church. This change at the home, talk of God's blessing at the local church, sends out a reverberation that has an effect far, far away. As far away as Moab!

The effect of Bethlehem's harvest is to disturb Naomi's grieving lethargy and cause her to think again of home—spiritual home! It also provides what she needs, the energy to rise out of the ashes of grief. Grief is like ashes. It represents something that no longer has substance, yet it can weigh us down to a different kind of death—spiritual death. Naomi feels the wave of God's moving in Bethlehem, Judah. Like Samson of old, she begins to think and feel again, not just the human desire to live but the believer's desire to walk with God and His people. So she must arise and take control of her life again. So does the backslidden believer!

They make the decision to get up out from the place where they are. It is not a full plan, not worked out from start to finish yet. But it is crystal clear as to what she must do. Naomi does not need to have a step-by-step daily process prepared. She certainly does not need a prewritten program. She does require obedience and an instant response in her heart to believe the good report, to arise and go, to return. She will find the gift of trust, to believe that God will somehow supply the milestones and the guideposts along the way. Naomi knows where she is going right now, and she knows the general direction, so she gets up and goes! Dear believer, you too know the general direction—it is towards the local church. Get up and go; believe again!

chapter fourteen

BEING REPENTANT

The two young women get up and go with Naomi. They went, as the Scriptures tell us, *"on the way."* Naomi discovers that she knows the way! The child of God, the real believer, instinctively knows the way back. So this is the initial journey out of Moab. Maybe just out of the area they are in to some junction that marks the end of their present neighbourhood, maybe the end of the city limits. Perhaps it is not merely a physical landmark. More likely it is the believers' point of no return. Believing Naomi knows this moment; believing Ruth knows it too. Does Orpah?

This point of decision, for or against believing, is a moment that is intense, intense for both believer and unbeliever faced with a challenge to faith. But tragically, they respond differently. The believer knows it is necessary to get out of the city of destruction. It is for the believer an imperative. His or her whole life and future and eternity hangs on this moment. The unbeliever finds an excuse, because the way forward does not offer the same appeal. He or she senses a pull back to the same old place where they were.

The Bible is very clear on how God views this choice. It is like *"a dog [returning] to his own vomit"* (Proverbs 26:11). Given that it's the language God's Word uses to describes Orpah's actions in returning, who would be an Orpah?

Somewhere along this road Naomi begins to think more clearly. As a result she stops to speak to her two daughters-in-law. In Naomi's mind, this will be their last walk together. They do not realize this. It all seems to be happening as they go.

Often as those who are out of the way make their way back to the Lord, conversations are required. Some difficult, some hard, some sad. Some matter of fact. All are essentially spiritual. They are the removal of "baggage." Anything that may hinder the progress of the return must be let go. It cannot be taken. It is like a return to the old narrow gate that Jesus talks about.

This journey for Naomi is therefore about herself! It is her journey. She must own it herself. She must be prepared to leave all and return. Though no one goes with her, there is now no turning back. No matter what is before her, there is no turning back. She's done with going the wrong way in life. She's going home.

This journey has a twofold character for Naomi. It is a physical journey. It is also a spiritual journey. So too for us in returning to the Lord we love. There are physical distances and real conversations that must happen. A real clearing of ourselves must be undertaken. There is a realism that grounds us when serious decisions are called for in life. Many today come to Christ and are not instructed about this emptying, yet it is a fundamental aspect of true repentance. They therefore spend years hobbling along the Christian life, weighed down with rubbish from the old life, wondering why *"the Highway of Holiness"* (Isaiah 35:8) is so cluttered.

We are privileged in this little book to be witness to Naomi's conversation with her daughters-in-law. Never doubt the pain and difficulty Naomi has embraced in this moment. There is nothing light or simple about it. There is no sense of freedom happening in her heart. The moment—or rather this whole time, from hearing of bread in Bethlehem to making the decision to go back and right till now as she speaks—is saturated by a humbling repentant heaviness.

Repentance is a change of heart. We are not attaching sin to Naomi. Repentance is a bigger concept than just "sin." We are not her judge; nor do we have, in this narrative, real evidence of sin in her life. But we do have evidence of a fundamental change of heart! This change that we are observing is godly repentance in practice.

We are not condemning Naomi. We are crediting Naomi with a beautiful example of a repentant change of heart! This heart,

Being Repentant

softened by grace and life's trials, this revived believing heart, is instantly concerned for those connected with it. Yet there is a determination, sometimes tending to an extreme, to deal with any potential problems before they arise. Nothing must hinder Naomi's fixed intention to return to Bethlehem, Judah.

She looks out for the good of her daughters-in-law, for their security. We will find no recriminations in her conversation with them. No harshness; just kind, giving words, words that cost only Naomi. The only negative effect of these words will be loss to herself. Loss of the very support and strength she prays for them! They will go back to family and friends in Moab. She will go on alone, and she feels this is a just loss to herself.

This repentant heart, the believing heart, is now exclusively dealing from a position of humble obedience to the will of God. All she says and decides, and all the decisions for others she makes, will be observed first between God and Naomi. Nothing will be done that will hurt this primary and essential relationship. "Though none go with me...no turning back." The old hymn is anonymous, but it was written by someone who had had Naomi's experience with God.

This is a new Naomi. This is a different Naomi. Naomi has had a meeting with God in her own heart. This dealing with the Lord Most High produces a decisiveness and a conviction that is clear and firm. It is the mindset of the believer. The heart has been touched, and it affects the mind in clarity of thought and direction, in values and truth. The mindset of believers is clear regarding where they are going and what they are prepared to leave behind—everything! Naomi knows what she is about to say, and its implications mean that she is going alone! She's emotional and loving and sad but determined and unflinching in her expectation of human solitude on her walk to Bethlehem, Judah. And so it is time for her to speak. Time to address issues that she cannot see a legitimate way around.

chapter fifteen
BEING TOO FOCUSED

And Naomi said to her two daughters-in-law, "Go, return each to her mother's house. The LORD deal kindly with you, as you have dealt with the dead and with me."
—Ruth 1:8

Naomi speaks to them both as to one. She has, without realizing it perhaps, assumed that they will both accept her reading of things. She also assumes that they will both react in exactly the same way to her proposal. But can we ever be so sure about the responses of individuals under duress? The pressure these three women are under is intense, both emotionally and practically. Anything is possible!

Nevertheless Naomi expresses her case as though it is clearly obvious to them both that they should just go back. She tells them that she has nothing to offer. No future, no life, and above all no young men to introduce as potential husbands. Naomi gives what she can. She gives them their freedom to leave her. She can only manage to express her pain by fashioning it into a prayer: "*The LORD deal kindly with you.*" She commends them for having been good wives to her two sons: "*As you have dealt with the dead.*" She's being kind in her words to avoid any sense that she's telling them she does not want them. She remains in a prayerful attitude and expands on her good desires for them.

However, there is a lesson here about being repentant. Repentance is focused but not solitary. It is not just one emotion. It is many. It is not one attitude; it is many. Not one mindset or one desire. Though it is intensely focused, it is not at all monolithic! It is dominated by self-examination. Often the individual has an admirable single-mindedness about the change of direction they see as necessary. Naomi, here, is going home. But we can drag into the rigid space of repentance other things that are in fact not at all rigid. From Naomi's perspective it is not possible for anyone to accompany her. But that is an issue for God to decide. It is not essentially part of Naomi's renewal, that she should return alone. Actually, we know from the rest of the narrative that in fact it is essential that Ruth does go with her. In fact God has moved Naomi for the primary purpose of taking Ruth to Bethlehem, Judah! Naomi cannot see this at all—yet!

Repentance should have the decisive full encompassing determination that Naomi shows. But repentance should also introduce a fundamental insecurity based upon a loss of confidence in self. Repentance and the desire for a new relationship with God should always have this insecurity. Naomi just might be a little too certain about her plans and be missing God's plans.

Strange as this may seem, this is a common failure in the genuinely repentant soul. Many people, set upon putting their life in order, make this mistake. They feel so clearly that the Lord is dealing with them. They sense they have been brought to a humble place. A listening place. The Lord's voice is becoming clearer when they read the Scriptures. He has been encouraging them since the day they returned to Him. They now have a good idea of what they need to do, have come to terms with any challenge involved, and are all wound up and ready to go! God is seldom finished teaching us when we feel we have learned the lesson!

The lesson for us is that listening to the Lord, getting right with God, is a continuous state for the believer. And also it is equally important to remember that this continuous repentant heart does not ensure safety from ourselves. We are arguably more at risk now than we were before. Before repentance, we knew we we're wrong; now we think we are right! And we are, but only for a brief moment. It must be carried through for a significant length of time,

Being Too Focused

until practice produces that beautiful repentant spirit as a habitual state of being. It is one of the most beautiful characteristics of the godly: they are in a continual state of consciousness about their own sinfulness, and this is balanced by an equally continual habit of repentance, coupled with joy in God's forgiveness and cleansing. They are also filled with a singular focus upon God and His people.

Naomi, fresh from her time of decision making, brimming with maternal love and tears, blunders in to declare her position. She has all the looks of a woman having taken control of her life and circumstances. She has it all worked out. She's going back to Bethlehem. Therefore they must also go back—to Moab? She's buoyant with purpose. It's all good. But any further input the Lord might have in mind is going to be a shock! Naomi has so quickly removed the Lord from the matter and taken full control herself. She needed Him to get her back on her feet, but now she has stopped listening. So quickly we go from listening to talking. So quickly we rise from humble learning to confident instructing.

Naomi has committed yet another common failing. She only sees matters from her own perspective. She forgets that in every affair of men, God is working out a greater plan. A higher aim is envisaged than our mundane existence! She will complete her speech, prepared or spontaneous, but it will not bring the clean conclusion she expected! God is doing something. Naomi is only a part. And she got it wrong despite her humility and total commitment to going back.

How guilty we are of accusing God of cruelty without realizing it! God had no intention of letting this dear child walk the walk alone. God seldom leaves us alone. He put men in families; He puts believers in families too, the church family. Neither did God intend to dispatch Ruth back to heathendom! What kind of good news is it that lets the saved soul fall back to lostness in Moab? That is no gospel at all! Naomi continues her speech, Ruth and Orpah will listen and respond individually. God will accomplish His plan. All despite Naomi's vigorous and genuine change of heart.

SECTION III:
BEING BROKEN TALK

chapter sixteen

THE GODLY GIVING BAD ADVICE

"The Lord grant that you may find rest, each in the house of her husband."

—Ruth 1:9

Naomi gives us help. She expands on the needs of these two young widows. She has been a widow for longer than they have. She can speak to them, and us, with the authority of experience. She wants the Lord to grant them—that is, give them freely—"rest." Rest is what they need. The rest of permanence and security. For Naomi this rest for them is best found *"each in the house of her husband."*

God in His interventions never only accomplishes one thing, even though the blessing in focus is directed to one specific thing. His blessings, while they reach the point of need, at the same time spill over beyond the initial need. The high priests' robes had pomegranates embroidered around the bottom edges of the garment (Exodus 28:33). These are not like the breastplate in significance, carrying the tribes of Israel into the holy place. They suggest this idea of blessings spilling out beyond the main fabric of the garment:

> *You shall make the robe of the ephod all blue...And upon its hem you shall make pomegranates of blue, purple, and scarlet, all around its hem, and bells of gold between them all around: a golden bell and a pomegranate, a golden bell and a pomegranate, upon the hem of the robe all around.*
> —Exodus 28:31–34

Being Ruth

The poor woman with the issue of blood in the Gospels discovered this for us (Matthew 9:21)! Even the edges of Jesus's garment conveyed blessing to her in the form of physical healing. Similarly here in our story, God will give a husband to Ruth. But He will do more than this. In the process of giving a husband to provide rest, He will further His eternal plan of salvation! That salvation will bring eternal rest to countless souls throughout eternity.

Naomi appears to feel useless, a failure. Life can be so cruel, even for the godly. See how a sense of failure reduces a person of worth to feeling worthless. It's a lie, but sadly, many worthy saints believe it! Naomi believed the lie that she was washed up, finished, and useless, like a piece of old, worn, and twisted wood on the beach.

Don't be like that! No child of God is ever useless—ever! Our God is a God of restoration, of new life, of new beginnings. He can accomplish things in us and through us greater even than in our successful years till now. *"Their sins and their lawless deeds I will remember no more"*! (Hebrews 10:17).

Jeremiah says, *"For I know the thoughts that I think toward you, says the LORD, thoughts of peace and not of evil, to give you a future and a hope"* (Jeremiah 29:11). He has plans for Naomi and for Ruth that Naomi's humbled repentant heart has discounted. It appears that her belief system is now at the level of miserly desperation. We can sympathize with this dear child of God considering the great sadness that has brought her to this place.

Orpah and Ruth both hear and understand Naomi. They know she's telling the truth. She has nothing to give at the human level, no resources, nothing left to offer. Orpah, like a fool, accepts this reading of Naomi. Ruth, like a believer, rejects it! Both understand her stark advice to go back to their own people. Orpah, like a fool, takes it. Ruth, like a believer, rejects it. Orpah, like a fool, looks after herself. Ruth, like a believer, looks after her neighbour, Naomi. For Ruth, this is not just about Naomi. It's about a way of being, being committed. Commitment is one of the great beauties in being godly.

Ruth has become a real believer. Though a proselyte, a convert to Judaism, she has been listening and learning and walking with the God of Israel for a significant number of years now. Possibly since she met Mahlon. Ruth must have discovered many things about walking with God. Her own time of bereavement and years of observing and listening to dear Naomi would have taught her a lot. But an early lesson she would have learned is that being godly involves putting others before yourself.

Jesus says this is a summary of the Law: "*And the second, like it, is this: 'You shall love your neighbor as yourself'*" (Mark 12:31). We see this as a beautiful characteristic of Naomi. It is also evident in Ruth. it's not just a natural trait. It has been worked into them in life by the Holy Spirit's sanctifying dealings. They have come through fire, and some real spiritual exercise, to arrive at this position. Orpah, as we observe, is distinctly different. So Ruth is not just going to do what she's told. Especially if it means going back to heathenism!

What was godly Naomi thinking? What kind of advice is this? It is the advice of desperation, from a godly woman who has just taken her eyes off the Lord! Naomi probably imagines she's understanding the will of God. She's certainly trying to deal with life wisely, even if it is painful for herself. But Ruth seems to have a better grasp of bigger principles at this point in the narrative.

See here how understanding godliness helps Ruth to understand what to do in a difficult situation. Often we want some revelation from God to solve a crisis. Ruth shows us that the guidance we may require is often already inside us. Being godly has taught Ruth how God works. God has shaped her into a committed person. Ruth loves Naomi, not just as a mother-in-law but just simply as her neighbour in life. There is no need for a revelation or guidance. Ruth is being who she is, a godly person. And she gets it right!

In Naomi's mind, she's going home imagining there is nothing else to be said. She expects a clean break with Ruth and Orpah. She has fully imagined the tearful moment to be the final separation. Then she expects a long, lonely walk. She's a woman to be pitied right now. But that does not excuse her failure in sending the daughter back to Moab! What is wrong with her?

Being Ruth

Well, her attitude is quite common in people who are genuinely trying to walk with God but have not fully let go of control of their own situation. Naomi's listening was too narrow. Too—dare we say—divinely focused? Such a tight form of listening to God can shut out the cry of the need staring at us.

Orpah has a focus: herself. She leaves Naomi in her pain. Naomi has too narrow a focus on God. She ignores Ruth's pain. Ruth, being godly, loves the Lord with all her heart, soul, mind, and strength, and her neighbour as herself. She has a beautiful concern for Naomi in her need.

We are all at times just like Naomi, allowing troubles to confuse our listening. But God knows how to get our ear!

SECTION IV:
TEARS

chapter seventeen

WEEPING BEING WEAK

> *"The Lord grant that you may find rest, each in the house of her husband." So she kissed them, and they lifted up their voices and wept.*
>
> —Ruth 1:9

The Discordant Trio

They lifted up their voices and wept. A sore moment for all of them. A seemingly hopeless end. Naomi kisses them. A kiss without falsehood or confusion. Simple, as in "singular," in its meaning. Totally wholesome and genuine in its pure affection. A gentle maternal expression that summed up her love for them both. Brief, and better than words.

We can see these three women holding each other and weeping freely as Naomi finished speaking. They fell on each other, lifted up their voices together. This passion can only be expressed by sobbing. It cannot be embarrassed or controlled in the moment. A discordant trio! An unresolved harmony! The notes E and D played together are jarring until resolved to E and C. Here they jar but without resolving, in an emotional outburst that took all the combined pain of famine past, death, widowhood, loss, and loneliness. All that had been stolen from them right until now, they engulfed with tears. It was a final anguished chorus.

Silence ensues. But on the balcony of heaven, they are watching—the Church triumphant—watching always, listening, waiting to see what this moment will produce, hoping for that resolve bringing the C to perfect harmony with the E. Because emotion itself is a disharmony, intangible until coupled with action. How often lives have been sucked dry by emotion!

It has little worth on its own. The tears. The kiss. The "I love you" cannot be grasped, must be questioned, doubted even, if it is not soon followed by action, perhaps by an "I do!" This moment is powerful nonetheless for these three. Powerfully hopeless. The moment is simply expressed in the secular song that says "There's no love song finer, but how strange the change from major to minor, every time we say goodbye."[6] That is the worldly man's summing up of sad goodbyes.

But in this story, God was right there for the believer in it all! Naomi's God. In the thick of all this agony—and agony it was. This triangle of struggle. Almighty God was right there at the centre of it all! He is always where we don't expect to find Him. And never distant or passive. He is active in all of it. Separate, yet engaged. Immersed, yet not polluted. Working, guiding, controlling—yes, even controlling chaos. Gently, never forcing, always spilling out grace and mercy and love, everywhere. Is He about to rise from His throne and come down? Not yet! Is He about to rescue a failed attempt at something? Never! He is not moved or shaken by all this mess. He is not worrying. He is just quietly being God.

Naomi has spoken. Expressions of human love and pain have all been exhausted. Naomi is packing it all up. She thinks she has just taken control. But she's about to realize she's not in control. Naomi has never been the one at the helm!

We often feel like this when we have moments of recommitment. We say we have given ourselves to the Lord, but we actually feel we are in control by so doing—we are not! Says Jesus, *"Take My yoke upon you"* (Matthew 11:29). He invites us to bind ourselves to Him and learn to be led by His controlling hand. We often think that our repentance and renewal are actually us taking a better

---

[6] "Ev'ry Time We Say Goodbye," lyrics by Cole Porter, Lyrics.com, STANDS4 LLC, 2019, *"Every Time We Say Goodbye Lyrics,"* accessed December 3, 2019, https://www.lyrics.com/lyric/16113245/Ella+Fitzgerald.

hold on ourselves, dealing with habits and failures and gaining disciplines and patterns of life. He says, *"Follow Me, and I will make you fishers of men"* (Matthew 4:19). This is altogether different! Naomi thinks she's in control; she's not—God is, always!

chapter eighteen

WORDS BEING WEAK

And they said to her, "Surely we will return with you to your people."

—Ruth 1:10

Ruth and Orpah, it seems, realize that Naomi is saying goodbye. Through the tears, they object. This, for them, is a terrible situation turning worse. Naomi cannot go on her own. *"Surely we will return with you."*

There are lessons to be observed in this exchange. Lessons about the dynamics of human conversations. Two good women assuring another good woman that they will stand by her, stay with her, go with her. Well, we understand that this was not necessarily what Naomi wanted. She had worked it all out. She had nothing to give them, and so there was no human purpose to be served in them returning with her. Indeed, it may well have presented a problem for Naomi. For example, how and where would they live? How would they feed themselves? A world of such questions had undoubtedly been considered by Naomi.

Naomi seems to think she has solved a problem. The response of the two daughters-in-law will dislodge her from her position into a disturbing confusion. How often our calculated sensible decisions are turned on their head by the Lord! The two women reject Naomi's position. *"Surely we will return with you."* Not quite what Naomi planned!

So we have come to know two young women after reading the book of Ruth. One, we know, will do the right thing. The other, we know, will not do the right thing. Both declare they will go with Naomi. Be warned—in this ancient exposure of emotional moments, emotions are shown to be weak! And so, even Ruth's protestation must be held in quiet abeyance. Held lightly, questioningly. Naomi's position is thought out, probably prayed over, and considered very thoroughly. Orpah and Ruth may not have imagined this scenario. Their responses cannot be accepted; they need to be tested. Emotional moments are not instantly trustworthy.

And so Naomi has met her first challenge to her plan to go back alone. Both daughters-in-law are coming with her! She's totally convinced that this is the wrong thing for them to do. How can she have arrived at this decision? We can easily see that practicalities alone supported her case. The believer needs more than mere practicalities or common sense to support serious moments in life.

Naomi has come a long way back in her spirit from when she was happy in Moab—if she ever was happy in Moab. That, we don't know. But her decision to return to Bethlehem is a clear sign of a closer walk with God. Nevertheless, it is seen to fail, in that there is still this sense of "I am in control"! That's not how the believer is to be. Nowhere are we in control! We are at best *"unprofitable servants"* (Luke 17:10). Servants are to do as they are told. We are called to follow Jesus, not run ahead of Him and do whatever we want. The right thing from where I am standing may be very different from what God sees as the right thing from His vantage point.

God is going to take Ruth to Bethlehem with Naomi. We are about to hear her plead a case for the wisdom of Ruth not going to Bethlehem. What's wrong? Naomi has just taken one step ahead of the Lord. She's so right in her general personal direction but so wrong about detail. She's doing what we all do. She gets half the message from God and then proceeds to fulfill the rest without Him.

Our typical acknowledgement in prayer of our great need and our lack of ability can so quickly be forgotten when we rise from our brief prayer time. We then feel free to use everything and anything that we think will work. Like Naomi here. Bethlehem? Absolutely! I will go! Such resolve is admirable when it is a resolve to listen to the Lord and let Him lead. But Naomi allows the Lord to give the general direction, and then she takes back the control of her life and begins working out the details herself! Naomi has not only met her first challenge; she has failed it. She's still not hearing the Lord. She's going to tell Him what needs to happen. The Lord has to invest a strong spirit in Ruth to overcome Naomi and her plans.

chapter nineteen

A SOUND CASE BEING WRONG

> But Naomi said, "Turn back, my daughters; why will you go with me? Are there still sons in my womb, that they may be your husbands? Turn back, my daughters, go—for I am too old to have a husband. If I should say I have hope, if I should have a husband tonight and should also bear sons, would you wait for them till they were grown? Would you restrain yourselves from having husbands? No, my daughters; for it grieves me very much for your sakes that the hand of the Lord has gone out against me!"
>
> —Ruth 1:11–13

Naomi's explanation has the realism of her time. It deals with the reality that life is universally hard for women. Naomi's life view is proven—not in a test tube or a lab or by a few thousand questionnaires but based upon real people everywhere throughout time. Including today. It is instantly recognizable anywhere in the world at any point in history. It has no relationship whatsoever to ideologies or social pressures. It is just the way life was then, and still is now. Naomi is without hope. She tells them plainly. But she is wrong, So wrong!

This moment in the narrative is sad. We thought famine in Bethlehem was sad. Then death superseded famine. Here we have hopelessness and loneliness. But that's not why it's sad! It's sad because it is a believer reading life without God. Life's message is never complete without Him. If believers look at life without God's active engagement in everything, they become the most miserable of all people. They still see all the problems. They are all still there. Removing God from our thinking does not remove problems; it only removes the solution. But unbelief has no rational to give comfort. No one is in control without God. Chaos can be our only expectation without God.

Without Christ we are without hope. *"If Christ is not risen, your faith is futile…If in this life only we have hope in Christ, we are of all men the most pitiable,"* says Paul (1 Corinthians 15:14–19). And again in Ephesians 2:12–13 Paul says, *"At that time you were without Christ, being aliens…having no hope and without God in the world. But now in Christ Jesus you who once were far off have been brought near by the blood of Christ."*

Naomi does credit "the Lord" with her circumstances, but only in as much as His *"hand…has gone out against me."* Of course she has a case she could argue. If Naomi ever argued with God about her circumstances, it is not recorded for us in the Bible. Here Naomi has simply come to the place of giving in reluctantly to the providence of God. She does not like it. She describes God as "against" her. Yet the teaching in the Bible about God's providence presents it as one of the most beautiful subjects. It tells us about God's care for us in His foresight of events and in His provision for these same events in advance, and in full, and all for our good. That's God's providence!

Naomi's repentance is now getting in the way of God's plans. Think about that. The good is often the enemy of the best! And why do we always credit God with the bad things that happen to us? We declare them confidently as His dealings with us due to our sins. Yet the good book of Job declares the opposite, at least in God's servant Job. Of course correction and chastening are loving fatherly events. But we can slip into a fake Christian misery that justifies our idleness.

Naomi may tell a half truth, or it may be the whole truth that God has gone out against her. But that in no way justifies her taking life into her own hands and ordering her affairs according to her own plans. Naomi is so busy planning her own providence that she has been systematically resisting God's providence. She is doing the right thing in going back to Bethlehem, Judah, even if it is reluctant and confused in her head and heart.

A Sound Case Being Wrong

She has reached an extreme the Lord did not intend for her in these circumstances. She thinks God is against her. God is never against the believer. The Lord is always out for our good. We might need to learn to be humble or any number of things, but His dealings are the dealings of a loving heavenly Father.

Naomi needs help. God is helping Naomi. Why is she fighting Him? Because she has moved ever so slightly away. She has loosened the yoke ever so slightly. It had become uncomfortable.

This breakdown happens all the time in churches and in the individual lives of God's people. We forget that our Christian life is not just about us. It is about God. God has a plan! It involves eternal issues. It is being worked out in a synapse between heaven and earth, between God and man, between good and evil, God and the devil. The plan is so much bigger than an individual, a famine, or a death. But we can begin to think it is all about us, plural. Or worse, all about me, singular!

Naomi has reduced God's plan to the size of herself! For Naomi right now, this little "church"—God and Naomi—is only as big as the walk from Moab to Bethlehem, and the only other "member" of that tiny church is the one Naomi told to leave and will soon refuse to speak to! Sounds sadly like many a tiny church in the modern world, and some big ones too.

But God is always in control, and Naomi will not have her way. Sending Ruth back in to Moab, sending believers back to the world—what a mess! Justified by human reasoning, caused by a thorough knowledge of the world but a diminishing knowledge of God's activity in the world. Our God is for us, not against us. So says Romans:

> *What then shall we say to these things? If God is for us, who can be against us? He who did not spare His own Son, but delivered Him up for us all, how shall He not with Him also freely give us all things?*
>
> —Romans 8:31–32

SECTION V:
BEING SPEECHES

chapter twenty

ORPAH BEING ORPAH

So, we have looked at all the people in the first half of the story. We have examined their names as a source of initial introduction. We can assume that the Holy Spirit inspired all the issues surrounding these people and that the information given is all in some way there to help us to learn lessons. We also understand that the book of Ruth is just one very small but essential part of the history of salvation.

Tragedies all have an end, often in one final blow. This part of the story is the final breakdown taking place. The initial family structure has its final rupture, and the last reduction is seen as Orpah takes herself back to Moab and to her gods.

> *Then they lifted up their voices and wept again; and Orpah kissed her mother-in-law, but Ruth clung to her.*
> —Ruth 1:14

A kiss was Orpah's final act. She had said she would go with Naomi. She had wept copious tears. We have reason to think that both her words and tears were fake, or at least self-deceiving. Perhaps she loved Naomi, but she loved herself more! The kiss failed. It was of all empty gestures the worst kind. Expressing affection of the deepest sort, then acting in total contradiction to all that a kiss suggests. A pathetic kiss, followed by a potent departure. Orpah left. How many women and fewer, but too many, men these days have felt the agony of this kiss? It does not qualify for the title "kiss." Like the best years of a partner's life, so is this kiss—stolen!

Let's deal with Orpah. The ancients can speak with such precision to us today. Orpah illustrates nothing new. Her kiss announces her departure, a kiss that cannot settle its gaze, cannot focus. It is looking away, to Moab. This kind of contradictory kiss is intended to be a hopeful gesture. The giver does their very best to make it real, but it is always fake! Perhaps worse than fake. It does nothing to help the person being left behind. Naomi is still alone! The real intention of this kiss is to silence Orpah's grinding conscience.

Conscience is annoying, but conscience has only little strength. Nevertheless it can silence Orpah's conscience in a moment. This kiss is like smoke—it has no substance but a bad taste. It can smother into a complicit silence an irritating conscience. Though gentle, it has a sting. This superficial gesture leaves permanent scar tissue. How many in our day have sold the Son of God for a such a kiss? So Orpah, in this story, and Judas, in the Gospels, take up this kiss and use it to sanction their hateful actions. Naomi is left alone, and the Son of God is crucified. A substantial shame remains with both Orpah and Judas all through the centuries.

Orpah is silently condemned by the narrative for forsaking the God of Israel, the only one and true God. She has chosen instead the dead stone idols of Moab. History has left evidence—in varying degrees of detail and quantity—sufficient to condemn the religions of that world and throughout the ancient world. Moab was not any worse than the other religions, but Judaism was amazingly more civilized and carried substance that produced a great nation and a great society. The other religions produced debauchery, not when they forsook their gods but when they practised their religion with devotion according to its stated beliefs. So a complete opposite effect to that of Israel.

The idea that all religions are about love is not accurate at all, even today. All religions want to be known as religions of love. But they cannot expunge their unholy books or their unholy histories, which declare clearly that they are religions of violence! Moab is recorded as using human sacrifices in its "religious" moments to appease the wrath of its god Chemosh.[7]

We see the end from the beginning. Orpah will walk away from Naomi, from her sister-in-law Ruth, and, sadly, from the God of Israel. She's returning to the familiar in the hope of gaining some control in her sad life. She has no heart for insecurity. "Insecurity" is her definition of *faith*.

What happened to Orpah? We do not know. Hopefully she found security and a purposeful life. Yet if she did, it was ordinary, at best, like most other young women in her day in Moab. She may have met disaster after disaster, but we do not know. Where is she? We do not know! She died centuries ago; so did Ruth and Naomi. Yet both Ruth and Naomi are very much alive in the pages of the Scriptures. Orpah kissed Naomi, but Ruth "*clung to her.*"

What a moment! Filled with contradicting emotions and confusing expressions. Naomi hoped it would be simple, but even the believer's life can be complicated and confusing. Orpah went back. The impression is that she walked away, there and then, after her "kiss." She walked away from both Naomi and Ruth and from the Lord.

---

[7] *Zondervan's Pictorial Bible Dictionary*, Merrill C. Tenney, gen. ed. (n.p.: Zondervan Publishing, n.d.), 153.

chapter twenty-one
NAOMI FAILING TO BE NAOMI

And she [Naomi] said, "Look, your sister-in-law has gone back to her people and to her gods; return after your sister-in-law."

—Ruth 1:15

This is how we know that Orpah rejected more than just her mother-in-law. Naomi says she has "gone back to her gods." Every decision needs to be looked at to see what the implications are. Orpah just wanted to go home, happy to be forgotten. But her empty kiss would remain. Held in a permanent written record. Suspended, timelessly mocking her. Naomi is blinded by certainty, all the while confident in her practicality.

Naomi now has an ally in Orpah's returning to Moab to support her case that Ruth should also leave. Beware when we must find support for our case in the world's attitudes, institutions, or people! In today's Church it is a common heresy. Listen to these conflicting words from a genuine repentant Naomi as she counsels Ruth to follow Orpah's example. Naomi then proceeds to speak to the matter. Exhausted by her troubles, she presents a compelling case for Ruth to go back to Moab.

Naomi uses Orpah as a lever to pressure Ruth to return, to also go back. She tells Ruth to look at what Orpah has done. To listen to what she's saying and go back. Even go back to your people and to your gods! Surely this is not Naomi speaking? Well, yes it is. But she's not speaking or acting like the Naomi we understand her to be! This Naomi, when she thinks she has just repented and returned to the Lord and is setting her life right, is making an awful lot of mistakes. If only she would let herself be the Naomi she is! But she's failing to be her true self.

This passage without Ruth would have condemned the book of Ruth into the mists of time, to be forgotten. It would have been just another story of the failure of Israel to do right, even in the individual and family. Every character in the book, so far, has failed abysmally. Naomi, our hope right now, the one we are looking to help us, is okay with Orpah's departure. Finally, the last blow, Naomi wants Ruth to follow Orpah back to Moab. Surely this is the lowest point in the book of Ruth? Everything is wrong! Everyone is wrong! Even God seems to have produced a monumental mess!

At this point the book has been reduced to morbid repetition. It is in danger of becoming just another monotonous story. The story of the depressing defeat of the human race by death and barrenness and unbelief. Worse, a defeat of the child of God.

At this point when we are ready to give up along with Naomi, Ruth speaks! Ecclesiastes says, *"There is...a time to speak"* (Ecclesiastes 3:1–7). What is this time? How do we recognize it? What is special about it? It is a holy vacuum. The vacuum was created by Naomi's morbidity. It has been expunged by the final removal of Orpah. For a moment it is now a still, pure place. God creates such times, before He intervenes, before He speaks into lives and situations. God is holy. Our place must be purified before He speaks. Before His presence is made known to us.

This holy vacuum attracts God. The empty space of our lives is improved by this sanctifying vacuum, but it is not satisfied by it. We need God to fill it. God often brings someone into the moment to speak. If no one senses it, recognizes it, hears its silent cry and responds to it, this moment of pure potential will refill itself with a fresh set of younger, more energetic demons, worse than the old ones.

Ruth is God's voice in the wilderness of this story. Ruth is the purifying voice of the Holy Spirit that will fill this vacuum with beautiful substantial godliness.

Ruth will fill the vacuum with godliness, a sanctifying influence. Indeed she will bring all the fullness of God back to the entire story of the book of Ruth. Ruth speaks, but she has no idea of how inspired her words will be.

chapter twenty-two

RUTH BECOMING RUTH

But Ruth said…

—Ruth 1:16

Ruth's passionate commitment is a high point, not only in this little book but in the whole of the Scriptures. It is conceived in the sheer agony of the moment. It is a spontaneous heart expression, the most pure and instant of utterances. Here it is, as such expressions often are, disarmingly beautiful. Many readers stop and weep. It is far too rich to be called a reply. It's not a thought-out thing! Thought processes, word structures, composition—these play no part. Pathos has the instant preparation of inspiration. Ruth's heart, not her head, formed these tender, vulnerable, and loving expressions. Here in God's Holy Word, they are boldly made public. Her statement powerfully refuses the pain felt from Naomi's appeal for her to leave.

Can there be a more empty place than that place where all you loved has died? The previous life is gone. To go back offers less than to go on, even into the unknown. But Ruth is not speaking to herself; she's looking at Naomi.

In Naomi there was a real glimmer of hope, hope founded in character and substance. There needs to be more than company, more than just someone to talk to. There needs to be godliness and personal depth to replace loss. Naomi had character. Her belief in the God of Abraham, Isaac, and Jacob was what had given her character and made her a substantial person. Believers ought to be people of a godly substance. Many are, and they do not realize it!

Naomi would never have described herself as such, yet Ruth saw it, and we see it. It is declared of her by Ruth's entreaty.

Consider this reality when the devil tempts you to give up, to go back to the world. The world degenerates; it does not regenerate. The world you left to go to Jesus is no longer there. It has been spoiled even more than when you were in it and unsatisfied by it.

The words Ruth delivers express the real believing heart when tempted to leave the God we love. This is the same heart expression as Simon Peter's when he said to Jesus, *"Lord, to whom shall we go? You have the words of eternal life"* (John 6:68).

But Ruth is not just rejecting the idea of going back. She's rejecting the suggestion of not going forward! She can't imagine life tomorrow without Naomi, whatever that tomorrow might bring. Her whole being has been fixed, and she only wishes to stay with Naomi, her mother-in-law. She also has no conception of "life" without the God of Israel.

You will find yourself returning to Ruth's words. You will not have to memorize them or frame them on a wall plaque. You will find them written on your own heart every time you need them. They are not poetry, but they are inspired. They are the inspired Word of God!

If the story thus far has been about loss, Ruth's statement has a timeless permanence. It gives. It ministers. It joins; it does not separate; it has united breaking hearts for centuries. Your own journey may have brought you to famine, but do not despair. God always has a way back.

Ruth's outpouring is also the bottom of a spiritual abyss that we all must reach if we would cling with similar conviction to the God we love. So propelled with heart conviction is Ruth's outburst that the journey back to Bethlehem appears to be accomplished despite a silent stand-off between these two. But however long it took and whatever words were exchanged or ignored, the silence became a sanctuary. God often bring us there, even against our will, to meet Him and to have the offering of our pain accepted, turned to worship, and made victorious over ourselves.

chapter twenty-three

DIVINE WORDS IN A WOMAN'S VOICE

A divine message is delivered here in a female voice. Soft and gentle. Firm. Not the thundering of the prophets. God does not always thunder, but He always speaks. Hear His voice at the end of yours. When you have no more to say, listen. Naomi has finished; He waits. God will not speak over you. He will sometimes silence you. He will let you speak your foolishness. Then, as in a still small voice, He speaks into your silence. He points us to the Lamb slain before the foundation of the world. He reveals His grace and His love gently to the hurting, to the hopeless believer, to the confused. He puts words in our mouth. The words that are lacking, He supplies. We could never frame them with such grandeur. Our words are ordinary even when we are ever so impressed by them.

Grand words come from Ruth but are God-given. Read them over and over again. Own them. Take them to yourself. They instantly fit every believing heart. Read them out loud, wherever you are; make them your speech; say them to the Lord—and never be the same again!

The Bible says, *"But Ruth said"* (Ruth 1:16). This is the moment of transformation in the book of Ruth. This is the moment of reversal. You feel that something extraordinary is about to happen. These words *"But Ruth said"* are among the best preludes ever penned, more beautiful than any one of Bach's "Well-Tempered Clavier."[8] They encapsulate all that is to come, and they declare the beginning of something new and better than what has gone before.

---

8 *Bach-Werke-Verzeichnis,* Wolfgang Schmieder, ed. (1950).

They are filled with anticipation, pregnant with hope. While the words are Ruth's, we sense that they are the inspired Word of God. They legitimize this book in its place in the canon of Holy Scripture.

"*But Ruth said.*"

If you cannot feel their depth in the spiritual realm, imagine them, for a moment, in the human realm. Make them the words of the partner about to leave but having changed position and, dispensing with the fake kiss, declaring Ruth's entreaty instead. Imagine then the great emotional dam that would burst; see the flood of tears filled with comfort and blessing. See a spouse prepared for abject loneliness but instead being embraced by a convincing commitment! Then see these words as God speaking to you. Make them also then your words to speak to Him.

SECTION VI:
RUTH SPEAKS; GOD SPEAKS

chapter twenty-four

THE ENTREATY

It is embarrassing enough for me to have assumed to write at all about this beautiful book. Who am I to hold such a trophy, let alone lift it high as though it were mine? To touch it overmuch would be more likely to pollute it than to enhance it. Yet anyone setting out to comment in speech or in writing upon God's Holy Word is faced with this sense of awe. The sinner, even the redeemed sinner, taking up things that are spotlessly holy cannot do so without a terrible sense of restraint.

So this particularly special quote from the book of Ruth is printed alone before any comment, so as to initially let Ruth speak, to let Ruth address the reader herself. These words are, of course, the very Word of God to everyone who reads them. This will be the shortest chapter in my book *Being Ruth*. May it please God to let it shine forth large and reach every reader's heart, moving us to fall at Jesus's feet and make such a commitment to Him.

> *But Ruth said,*
> *"Do not urge me to leave you*
> *or to return from following you.*
> *For where you go I will go,*
> *and where you lodge I will lodge.*
> *Your people shall be my people,*
> *and your God my God*
> *Where you die I will die,*
> *and there will I be buried.*

Being Ruth

*May the Lord do so to me and more also
if anything but death parts me from you."*
—Ruth 1:16–17 ESV

chapter twenty-five

BEING COMMITTED TO LOVE

Orpah is now silent. Naomi had a moment. Ruth is still speaking today. Love is in every syllable. But it is not a statement of love as such. It is a statement of absolute, determined commitment.

Commitment is a cold concept compared to love. But we should not set the one against the other. Here they coexist in perfect harmony. Commitment carries love deeper, longer. It is the depth and extent of this commitment that causes us to ponder. There is no need for academic examination. No need of language analysis. These words demand that we take ownership of them. Speak them to the Lord. Speak them to your loved ones. Speak them to your local church.

The reader feels the presence of the Holy Spirit in the words. Yet Ruth's words are thoroughly human and directed to Naomi. The diligent believer is looking for Christ in the Scriptures all the time without forcing God's Holy Word into our particular theological opinion and while avoiding the error of reshaping God's eternal Word to fit our earthly environment. Without "[*twisting the Scriptures*] *to [our] own destruction*" (2 Peter 3:16), can we find Christ in this Scripture in the book of Ruth? We certainly can.

Ruth's utterance is divinely inspired, included in the canon of Holy Scriptures and held safe for centuries. This tiny wee book has been defended and preserved from wicked powerful men who sought to burn it, tear it up, make it illegal to read or own. They have sought to destroy it, to silence it. Yet in the atheistic, evil Western world of the 21st century AD, the tiny wee book of Ruth is still being read! And it still speaks!

Ruth is still loved, admired, named after, emulated. Surely there is more to her story than herself? Surely the age-old interest to find Christ in the Scriptures honestly will reveal food for our souls. God makes every one of our lives about more than just ourselves but about Jesus every day. Why this intention, this search for Jesus Christ?

However good or loving or kind or self-giving, each of us—indeed all of us joined together—fails. Not even our corporately universal best can begin to approach the level of the tiniest particle of the stature of the man Jesus Christ, even if He were not divine!

Combine all the best of men. Call together and add up the merits of all the religious and irreligious "saints" of time. Of course we will have difficulty finding any "non-religious" saints, but assume that we can elevate a few good men, for argument's sake. They are all flawed and spoiled by blemishes and bruises, condemning spots and wrinkles. We can look upon each other's spots because we are all the same. Therefore judging among ourselves we are acceptable among ourselves but totally unacceptable to the eyes of divine perfection. But this man, even His enemies could *"[find] no fault in this Man"*—said by Pilate (Luke 23:14–15). Surely our search for Him is justified. So let's look at Ruth's entreaty.

chapter twenty-six

DO NOT URGE ME TO LEAVE YOU

"Don't urge me; do not pressure me with arguments or reasons, not even with emotions!" Naomi has presented a case for them to go back. Ruth will have none of it. She physically clings to Naomi and will neither go nor let her go until the very concept of separation is cut off. Even while Naomi spoke, Ruth had decided she would have none of it!

Naomi is speaking genuinely. She is older, more realistic, more honest, but sadly not expressing the mind of God, just her own thoughts out of her emptiness. We know this because we know that God wanted Ruth in Bethlehem, Judah, not Moab! Human reasoning and God's wisdom seldom unite and more often fight. And so note an aside about this passage. The elder, mature, lifetime-experienced servant of God is seen here to be corrected by the new convert. The one who should know does not know, and the one who should not know does know!

Naomi is wrong. Ruth is right. This is God's way of working often. He brings to nothing the things that are thought to be something so that no flesh can glory in His presence (1 Corinthians 1:28-29). Ruth bursts out with the most exquisite language, not even realizing it. Naomi—her speech is just all wrong! Her words are spiritually offensive! The thoughtful considerations of her dear experienced heart are just plain wrong! Poor Naomi! What has happened to her? If you know someone like this pray for them; don't condemn them!

Ruth is helping Naomi. Naomi is speaking out of a broken spirit. An exhausted heart. She's bewildered by what has happened to her to this day and even this day! She simply does not know what to do. So she leans on her old experience of life. She has given up on finding the Lord in all this. She's giving up. She is, however, going back to Bethlehem the House of Bread. And her heart attitude is to get right with God. To soak up any pain that might still be necessary for her repentance to be full, she will find a humble place and sit quietly until this *"indignation is past"* (Isaiah 26:20). Until God's judgments have passed over, and peace returns.

Whatever we may say about Naomi in this painful moment, remember that in a few more days we will meet again the Naomi we have come to love and whose faults noted here will all be forgotten. Naomi and Ruth will be best friends again, speaking the same language and walking in the same blessing of God, together. But there will be no going back to Moab!

We can find ourselves very far off the mark when we have been hurt or are dried up or weary. Naomi should *"Stand still, and see the salvation of the LORD"* (Exodus 14:13). When you reach this place that Naomi finds herself in, do not despair. God is doing something! You can still rise again; you will stand again, speak again, and minister life again. Naomi gets there! So can you! And it was only just a few days walk to Bethlehem and bread. Encourage yourself. "I will not leave you," says Ruth, and so says the Lord to every troubled believer.

Here the Old Testament saint points us to New Testament words. Among the dearest of words, from the mouth of God Himself: *"For He Himself has said, 'I will never leave you nor forsake you'"* (Hebrews 13:5). Hear them. He is still speaking them daily in our hearts. Every time we pull against that *"yoke"* of Matthew 11:29, we will hear them, if we listen! Every time we struggle to go our own way, He echoes these words of Ruth: *"Do not urge me to leave you"* (Ruth 1:16 ESV).

We may not see our wanderings as this. But to the Lord, we are pushing Him away. He will have none of it! He tells us plainly, "I will not leave you!" And even when we drag and stretch that yoke, it never breaks. It is resilient, He is resilient—dare I say like Ruth is resilient? Of course it's the other way around! Ruth says this to Naomi, but God is refusing to leave her! God is staying with Naomi in the presence of Ruth. Ruth's words are God's words to Naomi. Naomi, who right now feels so alone, rejected, and forsaken. *"[God] has gone out against me,"* she says (Ruth 1:13), but God is right beside her, declaring His absolute commitment in the words of Ruth.

These words are for every reader to feel in their full emotional and practical force. He never goes back on His commitment! This teaching in the Bible is surely of absolute divine origin. It embodies the most profound revelation of God's character and a similarly profound revelation about the sinner's lack of character. Ruth here shows what godly commitment looks like. It is in the character of God to keep His word when He makes a commitment. We are not able to commit to Him in our own strength. God's commitment to us, not our commitment to Him, is the assurance of what is so rightly called our Eternal Security. In Christ the believer who has committed his or her soul to Jesus Christ for salvation is secure because God will never forsake His own Word. He promised to save us, and He will, right through into eternal life in Heaven. His commitment is based upon the work of Jesus on the cross for us.

chapter twenty-seven

OR TO RETURN FROM FOLLOWING YOU

They had walked out of the district they lived in. They had walked to the edge of town. The road that led to the country around Bethlehem lay before them. Ruth was not going back to Moab. We are surely to consider why.

Is it not because Ruth has come to believe in Naomi's God, the God of Israel? She has learned and understood a lot about Him over these past ten years or so. She certainly has discovered that He does not always keep us from trouble. Naomi lost her husband early! So did Ruth. But Naomi exemplified the strength of the believer in weakness.

Ruth took it all in. She must have seen evidence in the life of Naomi that convinced her that this God was real, so much so that Ruth will follow Naomi wherever she wants to go. What Naomi has is so attractive that Ruth will give up her home and family and country to keep Naomi. She's a "follower." Is this not New Testament language? *"Follow Me, and I will make you fishers of men,"* says Jesus (Matthew 4:19). They do, and He does! He makes them! Followers of Jesus are being changed, being made into something different.

But she must also have experienced the Lord herself, since she came to Him and accepted His rule, as God, in her life. So whatever the circumstance were that brought her thus far, she's not going back to her old life! She's not going to leave Naomi. Such is the attitude of the person who has come to trust in Jesus Christ for their salvation. They will not turn their backs on Jesus, no matter what circumstances He takes them into.

This refusal to go back to Moab is the evidence of a new life within! It is the evidence of a life that has been set free from bondage to this world. The old life has been left behind in Moab. She has committed herself to leave it behind.

The new believer has just been called out of this evil world. Therefore the idea of going back into it is understood correctly to be bad. Like Israel having been delivered by God's mighty hand out of Egyptian bondage but wanting to go back is seen rightly as a horrendous mistake! Yet for the believer who has fallen back into the old worldly ways of sin, going back is a return to the Lord. The phrase *going back* can mean a good thing or a bad thing.

For Ruth, going back is bad, while for Naomi, going back to Bethlehem, Judah, is to be understood as good.

Ruth says, "*Do not urge me to leave you*" (Ruth 1:16 ESV). The challenge to go back to the world is also a challenge to stop following Jesus. It is a common challenge in Christian experience. The Church does not seem to acknowledge this reality like it used to. So we do not prepare new converts for this spiritual fight. Many fail before they have even begun! Every profession of faith in Jesus is tested to see if the faith declared is genuine faith. A trial, a difficulty, a loss, a hurt—whatever it is, its purpose is to put to test this initial declared faith. To see if the new believer is really intent upon following Jesus and not going back to the old life. Real, genuine faith prefers and chooses the company of Jesus against the company in the world.

chapter twenty-eight
WHERE YOU GO I WILL GO

The Holy Spirit, in inspiring God's Holy Word for God's people through time, has made Ruth's words timeless.

Ruth is going on a spiritual pilgrimage. She intends to take a journey. You can't take everything you own on a journey; some things must be left behind. Journeys force a new set of priorities regarding what and who is important. She understands that this commitment includes a commitment to a certain type of place, and so she assures Naomi that this matter of "place" is settled in her heart. *"Where you go I will go"* (Ruth 1:16 ESV).

God is looking for such to come to Jesus, to go with Jesus! Every immigrant to North America made such a decision. They chose between home, family, country, friends, and familiar to go to an unknown world and people they did not know. But to stay was regarded as loss! This immigrant spirit is like the spirit of the Church. We have left all to follow Jesus.

The place we want to be is where God's people are. That is where God is, in the most basic sense. So Ruth commits to *"wherever you go."* Even though she has no real understanding of where this Bethlehem, Judah, is or what it is, she takes wherever Naomi goes as her starting point.

See the character of her commitment. It is exclusively to Naomi. It is universal in its geographical, social, and cultural scope. It is active in its daily application. It carries no self-interest, though it does hope for companionship, for reciprocation, for fellowship! But it is not about benefits. It is not grasping. It is giving—it gives everything! Here it is made from one woman to another, and it is one-sided, and it comes up against a resistance! Still Ruth carries on with her "declaration of commitment," but it is not marriage or a statement generated by emotional love. It is certainly not physical. But it certainly includes a pure physical commitment. "*Wherever you go, I will go*" is about a "place" in every sense of the word.

This conversation is coveted by every human heart. Express it how you will, the essence of Ruth's first few words is what the human heart longs for. We all want someone to make such a commitment to us and keep it! This is the way we are made. We need such closeness in life and in eternity. We are not made to be alone. We can survive alone—never doubt it! But we are not made to be alone. This it is not a marriage, and it is not a physical relationship as such, but it is a similar level of commitment. The Old Testament pictures the New Testament ideas. Here the idea of following, of committing your life, to Jesus is being exhibited in Ruth's commitment to Naomi.

When Jesus says, "*Come to Me*" (Matthew 11:28), you must leave where you are and go to Him! You must leave behind your old world. That is initially in terms of its place in your heart and mind, its principles and practices, its way of being, of seeing. Its culture. Often even physical places must be forsaken due to some evil intent. Sadly, but often, we must leave people too. People who refuse us in our new life. Because all these things are contrary to the new way of being that is what this series is about, being believers. But the emphasis is not on what we must leave behind; the emphasis is positive. "*Come to Me*," says Jesus. Ruth leaves Moab but finds Naomi, and that's just the beginning of her story!

The message is to go somewhere—to Jesus. When you get there, never go back to where you were before. He will never leave you; don't ever leave Him! Ruth has made it clear that she is not leaving Naomi or going back to Moab. She continues to spell it out for us. She says, "*Wherever you go, I will go*." And it's a universal and exclusive commitment.

"Wherever you go" is a geographically large commitment. Jesus Christ expects the same detachment from His followers. All our comfort zones regarding climate and beauty and familiarity—to say nothing of our sense of belonging—all of it is taken and laid on the altar of God. Nothing left out. "Wherever you go"—this "wherever" is the world.

The Lord may leave you exactly where you are geographically. But His aim is to take you to heaven, eventually, to be with Him. In this life, believers must set their eyes, like pilgrims, towards heaven. This effectively breaks the tie with all else in between. There will be stopping places on the journey. Whether few or many, none must attach themselves to us to the extent that they hinder our sense of pilgrimage. We are, as Hebrews says, *"strangers and pilgrims"* (Hebrews 11:13) in this world. Ruth shows us this character of the godly believer who perseveres and will not go back when faced with trials.

What would you look like if this sense of detachment was who you were in this world? How would you read the news? Would you read the news at all? How would you regard your home? Fixed—I like it and will never leave it? Or, it's just a tent; I can leave it anytime? How would you deal with your finances, investments, savings, and spending if you were a pilgrim passing through the world? We must be being believers in the world in everything. Citizenship of heaven is more important than citizenship of even the best country in the world.

Right now in this narrative Ruth's citizenship is out there, in the "wherever." She has such a New Testament mentality. Yet Abraham, in the Old Testament, was the same, was he not? *"And [Abraham] went out, not knowing where he was going"* (Hebrews 11:8). See Jesus's disciples: they were sent *"into all the world"* (Mark 16:15). So this godly faith that goes purposefully into the "wherever" is a tangible connection between the people of God throughout the ages. It is not new. It carried the gold dust of antiquity even in Ruth's day. Ruth says, *"Wherever you go, I will go."*

chapter twenty-nine

WHERE YOU LODGE I WILL LODGE

One of life's first concerns is shelter, the place we lodge in. For Ruth it is not about the shape, size, or quality of a building it's about a person: Naomi. Where she is—that's where Ruth is going, and there appears to be no need for more detail. Ruth had at least one house in Moab. She left it all behind and walked away as far as the road to Bethlehem, Judah. Here she gives it all up fully. This says something about her sense of priorities.

Paul says, "*For we who are in this tent groan*" (2 Corinthians 5:4), indicating his loose connection with everything in this world. He is talking about his body, which he calls "*this tent.*" He groans because he is tired of its constraints. It ties him down, it restricts him, and it has a tendency to take him away from the Lord. So do our houses, legitimate as they are.

For the believer, the case against owning a house is very thin, but it's not to be discounted out of hand. Few pilgrims in foreign lands own property! Only those who have settled in the land buy homes. Why have all that burden if you are moving on, not staying there for long, certainly not forever? And if you already have a home in another place and that is where you are heading to on this pilgrimage, why would you buy a property for a few short years? These are some of the reasons for some past believers not owning fixed things in this alien world. Nobody today is going to accept such a primitive idea, even if it reflects the Bible idea of pilgrimage. But to stop and consider the idea of a being pilgrim and living in tents might just set our minds free in such a materialistic day as ours.

Being Ruth

Learn to be like Ruth, who is prepared to go where Naomi goes and live where Naomi lives. Will you be like her and say to the Lord, "Wherever you lodge, I will lodge"? These kind of ideas take today's gospel and lift it into an older, more spiritually alert, more biblical gospel. Many today imagine that such commitment is for young people, not for those who have settled down, yet it is applicable to all of us for all of our days. Our lodging is in heaven.

Yet Ruth takes it even further; she continues as if Naomi needs to hear more. Was there a surprised look on Naomi's face? Should there have been? Should Naomi have expected godly Ruth to go back to heathen Moab? Surely not! Yet it appears that Naomi was not expecting this level of godly commitment from Ruth. Perhaps Ruth realized that Naomi was reluctant to listen, and so she continued.

chapter thirty

YOUR PEOPLE SHALL BE MY PEOPLE

> *"Do not urge me to leave you or to return from following you. For where you go I will go, and where you lodge I will lodge. Your people shall be my people, and your God my God"*
>
> —Ruth 1:16 ESV

"*Your people shall be my people*": People, people, people! How many people did Ruth have as relatives, friends, and acquaintances in Moab? She had probably spoken to them the day before. The previous week she was perhaps in their homes, talking and sharing with them. Were her parents alive at this time? We do not know. Had she brothers or sisters? We do not know! The Bible notably considers this information irrelevant. Naomi's people will from now on be Ruth's people. This is an affirmation of a new affiliation.

We cannot allow ourselves to be naive here and imagine that Ruth was a lonely, isolated, sad person. Would you not have liked Ruth? Who would not have liked her? She undoubtedly had a "people" of her own in Moab! And here we read that she's leaving them to go and be one with Naomi's people.

What makes Ruth here any less callous than Orpah? Is this not the same attitude as Orpah but in a different direction? No it is not! Because Orpah is at liberty to choose between friends. Surely this is a basic principle in normal human relationships.

Ruth's choice is not, ultimately, between Moabites and Israelites. Her choice is between this living God and those dead gods of Moab. This choice is what Ruth is about to express to Naomi. Right now she's coming to it via other subjects. Look again at her words: she tells Naomi, "*Do not urge me to leave you or to return from following you,*" and she then expands on that basic point. Here is what she means by that: "*Where you go I will go; and where you lodge, I will lodge. Your people shall be my people*" (Ruth 1:16 ESV). This takes us to the fundamental change that has occurred in Ruth: "*Your God [will be] my God*"! It is this choice that has brought Ruth to this declaration. Naomi's people will be Ruth's people because they are the people of God. Choosing God brings with Him many other great blessings: "*you...who once were not a people...are now the people of God*" (1 Peter 2:9–10).

Naomi was not thinking about religion when she pointed Ruth and Orpah back to Moab. Naomi was thinking about blood ties, human relationships, and mere friendship and help. This perhaps could explain the strange contradiction in what she believed and the advice she gave to her daughters-in-law, advice that strains everything an Israelite believes. We excuse Naomi as being under tremendous strain. She is worn and confused with the endless trouble she had known in Moab. She is only now coming to her spiritual senses and determined to go home. Home, remember, for Naomi is not just Bethlehem, Judah; it is God's people, the God of her fathers, the God of Abraham, Isaac, and Jacob, the God of the Exodus and the Ten Commandments. For Naomi, this is an inbuilt understanding, cultural conditioning of the best sort. It is who she has been since birth. Moab was a sad time, an aberration, for this family.

But for Ruth, this God, this promised land, this relationship—it's all new. For her it carries a freshness and joy that she will not let go. Darkness is her cultural background with cruel man-made gods of stone who suppressed them. The God of Israel, Jehovah God, Naomi's God, won her heart, and she is bound to Him now with ties that she can only see in terms of Naomi and her people. There is no way Ruth is going to give up Naomi, because she represents all that she has come to know in this wonderful, awesome, good God, Jehovah God.

The acknowledgement of Jehovah God intimates a priority above all other priorities. Some others may remain, but only in subordination to this first choice. Leaving one "people" for another is a consequence of choosing the living God. Orpah also chose between peoples. She chose her own people and therefore the stone gods of Moab.

The Christian case is still the same in its implications for our circle of friends. It may not result in us leaving town or refusing to visit our parents or cousins. But it undeniably introduces an eternal priority that cannot be ignored without serious consequences. So this matter of choosing people is really an offshoot of our choice between true religion and the true God and false religion and false gods. Ruth goes on in her entreaty to declare the central issue for refusing to return to Moab. The final and key issue is God.

chapter thirty-one

AND YOUR GOD MY GOD

"*Do not urge me to leave you or to return from following you. For where you go I will go, and where you lodge I will lodge. Your people shall be my people, and your God my God.*"

—Ruth 1:16 ESV

"*And your God my God*": This is the point Ruth has been working towards in her statement. She has not merely become religious. She has not merely chosen another god, a new god to her but just like the gods in Moab. She has not added something to a list of things already there. She was never an atheist. That would have been very unusual in history—actually, in any era until recent times, and even now.

Believers in some god have always been the majority in the world. It is arguably the case that there never was a world where real atheists were the majority. The Romans called the Christians atheists because they rejected the range of gods Rome had, and the Christians only wanted one God! There is a famous case in Church history illustrating this accusation, calling the believers atheists.

> Therefore, when [Polycarp] was brought before him, the proconsul asked if he were Polycarp [circa AD 69–155]. And when he confessed that he was, the proconsul tried to persuade him to recant, saying, "Have respect for your age," and other such things as they are accustomed to say: "Swear by the Genius [guardian spirit] of Caesar. Repent. Say, 'Away with the

atheists!'" So Polycarp solemnly looked at the whole crowd of lawless heathen who were in the stadium, motioned toward them with his hand, and then (groaning as he looked up to heaven) said, "Away with the atheists!"[9]

Similar charges of "atheism" and "impiety" were brought against Christians in Lyons in France in the 170s AD.[10] The perception of early Christians as atheists was not uncommon.

Ruth does not say "I will follow your God." She says, "*Your God [shall be] my God.*" Generations of the children of Christian homes have adopted their parents' religious beliefs without ever ratifying them in their own hearts. When this is not challenged, the beliefs of the churches are watered down. They are not guarded or fought for. Second generation Christians often do not know why they believe any of the things they believe. They cannot give a reason for their faith. Or if they can it is often bookish, unconvincing, a mere set of objective truths. What is too frequently lacking is this personal convincing experience that Ruth evidences clearly.

Parents are often so relieved that their children come to church that they never say anything to challenge them in case they frighten the youngsters away. We do not get to heaven by attending church or playing in the worship team or even being the pastor! We get to heaven by believing in Jesus as our own resurrected Lord and Saviour. And in the teaching of the Word of God, young believers must be tested. Ruth here is being tested. Parents must be brave enough to let this happen.

Our convictions may look the same as our parents', but they must become our own convictions in reality. Then our second generations or our Sunday school class children will be a force to be reckoned with in this world. Too often they are frightened, faceless people, in the world and even in the Church itself.

---

9 J. B. Lightfoot and J. R. Harmer, trans., *The Apostolic Fathers*, rev. Michael W. Holmes (Grand Rapids: Baker Academic, 1992), Mart. Poly. 9.2.
10 See H. Musiurillo, *Acts of the Christian Martyrs* (Oxford: Clarendon Press, 1972), 64–65.

Can you imagine Ruth being afraid to speak out about the Lord or about her faith in Him? Difficult to imagine, after this outburst of rejection—rejection of Moab's gods—and her bold and clear final commitment, to Naomi's God as "*my God.*"

Never fear trials of faith for your children. God has promised, and He will uphold them and deliver them stronger than before. Ruth is not finished; she has more to say about this faith in God and love for Naomi.

chapter thirty-two

WHERE YOU DIE I WILL DIE

"Where you die I will die, and there will I be buried. May the LORD do so to me and more also if anything but death parts me from you."
—Ruth 1:17 ESV

"*Where you die I will die*": Here Ruth reminds us that commitment in certain cases is understood to be for life. It is until we die.

Not every type of commitment has to be lifelong. For example, a company offering you a job today, while it needs some level of commitment to function, will not require a slavish lifelong loyalty. Nor would a particular political ideology. It is understood that our thinking on these issues can change because these areas of life are not permanent.

Marriage has always been understood as a lifelong commitment between one man and one woman. Yet many marriages break down and fail. It is a failure! It is a breaking! And it does untold damage to the human spirit, and to whole communities, every time it is broken. We are getting to a place where many think that we are just not able to keep that level of commitment. We certainly are able! We are human beings and no different fundamentally to any other human in history. And marriage has not failed. Marriage, for all the attacks of modern media, is still in normal conversation understood to be lifelong. It is still seen as a massive blow when it fails, indeed, the longer it has lasted, the greater the failure.

Breaking such a commitment leaves the individuals permanently damaged, often unable to ever trust again, even themselves. It robs people of a fundamental aspect of their human dignity. It is a noble thing to make a commitment like Ruth did. At the same time it illustrates for us our fallen humanity. Ruth says, "*Where you die I will die.*" That is a lifelong commitment. Ruth kept it, and so can we.

chapter thirty-three

AND THERE WILL I BE BURIED

> *"Where you die I will die, and there will I be buried. May the LORD do so to me and more also if anything but death parts me from you."*
>
> —Ruth 1:17 ESV

"*And there will I be buried*": Here we have the sense of place again. Is that so important? There is a gospel truth concealed in these words that is worth digging for. See the Christian teaching on baptism—being buried with Christ and rising with Him to newness of life. The believer is seen to be "in Christ" at His death and is also seen to be raised with Him in resurrection. The closeness, the oneness, the sense of being together permanently is what Ruth is expressing. It is also the teaching of baptism, that we are "in Christ."

The idea of the grave being our "final resting place" is supported by countless generations who have used the phrase or at least viewed the grave as such and reverenced it for generations of ancestors. The need is for a specific, permanent place where they will no longer be disturbed. An identifiable grave, as in a plot of ground or a cave or something similar. A place where loved ones can relate to the deceased, by either visiting or merely knowing its location. The grave is not for the benefit of the dead person. It enables us, the living, to be human in expressing continuing love, dignity, and respect for our dead.

Ruth will leave evidence at her death to testify to a life of commitment. She will be buried in the same place as Naomi. Ruth will so embrace Naomi that she will remain with her forever, in earthly terms, buried beside her. Ruth has time sorted out in her head and on her heart. Her life will be with Naomi, whatever else may happen. Can she say any more? Is there another point to make here? Surely she has said more than enough. No, Ruth has more to say!

She will round of her life of commitment having spoken to it in all its expressions. Commitment in every aspect is covered, but Ruth here will add a final comment so that with dignity, having run the race, she might finish the course and like Paul receive a crown of life! Ruth's end will be beside Naomi and in that grave, whatever form it takes. It will declare her commitment for all men to see.

So is there any more needing to be said on this subject of Ruth going with her to Bethlehem, Judah? One might think there is no more to be said. However Ruth sets her position finally, not here on the earth or in the memories of men but before God. The whole matter for Ruth is religious, is spiritual, is related to God. He is the fundamental part of all of this, for Ruth the Moabitess, convert to Israel. She will let Him have the final word.

chapter thirty-four

THE LORD DO SO TO ME AND MORE ALSO IF ANYTHING BUT DEATH PARTS ME FROM YOU

"Where you die, I will die and there will I be buried. May the LORD do so to me and more also if anything but death parts me from you."

—Ruth 1:17 ESV

"*May the LORD do so to me and more also if anything but death parts me from you*": Commitment to one another is a natural result of believing in a God who commits Himself to us. Ruth exemplifies this beauty of being godly. But Ruth is not just repeating herself. This is not some religious benediction she is adding. No, she's adding a curse upon herself. If she fails to keep her word, the Lord is to be her judge, and He has to actively do something about it.

This phrase "The LORD do so to me" is a form of expression used throughout the Old Testament. It is like a curse. It means "May God punish me in the same way as I have hurt you." Here the particular "hurt" Ruth is referring to is leaving Naomi before she dies. "May God do even more hurt to me than I would do to you if I left you." Ruth's expression pushes vocabulary to the furthest extent of her ability, her culture, and her religious understandings, involving the basics of life, keeping your word, and the essentials of a life walking with God.

It also calls on the highest power she can invoke. If her leaving Naomi brings any specific circumstances that damage Naomi, God is to mete out the same pain to Ruth. And "more also"! Ah, is this only if Ruth does something really bad? No, "if *anything* but death parts you and me"! Anything serous and anything trivial and all things in between. Was there ever a more comprehensive commitment?

The book of Ruth would not have been written if she had failed in her commitment. This is the case because the gospel hope would also have come to an abrupt and insignificant end. Of course it was not going to fail! We know the end of the story. Ruth is essential to that story, and God put in her heart the ideals necessary for the fulfillment of His divine plans in the lives of His servants. Ruth has blessed the world with this magnificent example of what a real commitment looks like.

It is time we raised the bar on commitment. It is time the Church set an example, as Ruth does here, to the world and before God. Then perhaps our word will be our bond again.

Ruth succeeded in making her point. But is Naomi happy? Perhaps not! Here, it could be that the Scriptures order a silence to follow, out of reverence for the beautiful godly words of Ruth.

chapter thirty-five

THE SILENT WALK

When she [Naomi] saw that she [Ruth] was determined to go with her, she stopped speaking to her.
—Ruth 1:18

Ruth speaks with more than words, as a woman determined in her mind. She's visibly expressing her intentions above her words. Naomi "saw" that Ruth was determined. Words are often insufficient to convince people. God "gave" His Son (John 3:16), illustrating His commitment to redeem for Himself a people, the Church.

However, here we have one of the most remarkable silences in the Bible. It appears that silence separated them like a wall. Ruth was so determined in her manner that Naomi just stopped speaking to her. We can understand why she stopped reasoning with her. But she stopped speaking to her? What was Naomi thinking, feeling?

Naomi is a broken woman. Silence is the only weapon she has left. No words. No advice. No small talk. No idle chit-chat. Certainly no smiles, and right now there is nothing in the world that is funny. Feigned laughing to lighten the atmosphere and make the best of a difficult moment—not a chance! Perhaps not even a smile. That is what the text seems to suggest. It is hard to imagine that the silence did not ease for a moment now and again. However the tension seems to have shut down all communication.

Silence is often the end of our human experience. We can shout and struggle and argue and reason. We can even fight with words and gestures combined, but when all fails, silence indicates our defeat. Here Ruth is not defeated or interested in winning anything.

But Naomi is in a bewildered, helpless depression, and it would appear to be loudly expressed by a sullen silence.

> *Now the two of them went until they came to Bethlehem. And it happened, when they had come to Bethlehem, that all the city was excited because of them; and the women said, "Is this Naomi?"*
>
> —Ruth 1:19

Why does the Bible not save itself some valuable word space? This sentence could have read, "Now *they* went until..." Surely a wise reduction in wordage, in a book that had to be small. Is it telling us that there was an emotional distance between them? That at the very time they most needed to be "one," they remained two separate people? This expression "the two of them" may well indicate that the two women never became "one," even as the journey progressed. Visibly separated by an invisible silence.

It is quite easy to imagine that this silence lasted for a significant time. Naomi was upset. Maybe they just did not know what to say. They were walking through mountainous terrain, on rough roads. Silence might, in fact, have been the norm. Walking and talking can be exhausting. It can also be invigorating, depending on the conversation, but Naomi was not in a place to offer anything invigorating!

Naomi still seems out of sorts when they get to Bethlehem, still miserable. Sad thoughts crowd her tired mind. Perhaps a relative will take her in, but now she is two! How will she feed herself, let alone Ruth as well? Where will she lodge? All the same questions every culture in the history of mankind asked. Someone will surely help her. But somewhere deep in the dark places of her heart, a tiny light points upward. Hour after hour, hill after hill, it presses to shine a light on her darkness.

By the time they get to Bethlehem, Naomi has moved only a little. She's talking about the Lord—but still talking about Him as though He were her enemy! She's not resisting His chastening, but not rejoicing in it either. This enforced silence may however have been a good rest for Naomi.

Surely many of us have been in that depths of despair. We have walked that long walk. We have found the Lord—and He helped us! Naomi needed that time to reflect. To pray and find herself and then to find the Lord.

Have you ever walked a problem off? Walking is a very healthy form of stress relief. Many of the great saints prayed as they walked. Many a mountain path is littered with problems and pains left behind by weary legs and troubled minds. The deep breathing of the upward journey can open up more than our lungs. The mountaintop gives us a superficial but perhaps useful feeling of being closer to God. Taken too far, we merely become animistic and unintentionally credit nature with the ability to reveal truth beyond its limited capacity. Nature declares that God exists; it shows His glory; but it cannot tell us about His saving grace through Jesus Christ. Today, if we are in need of a dealing with God, Jesus is where we need to go!

The walk might help these two women, both individually, to grow closer to the Lord. They will have some time. But they will not find God inside themselves or on a mountaintop either. They will find Him when He chooses to open their eyes and hearts to Him and to one another.

The Bible does not record any conversation between Naomi and Ruth on the walk. This may confirm our thought that these two were separated by silence. At Bethlehem, Naomi is forced to speak. As they get close she seems to have gotten herself into a better place, even if it is still a miserable space.

Ruth, was certainly being tested on her "declaration of intent." Would you have stayed? Did she never once reconsider in the silence? If she did, she rejected it and walked with a more definite step behind Naomi. What a woman! Surely going back to Moab would have been an easier road. But it's often the hard road that takes us to the people of God. This is where Naomi was going.

One way or another, they come to Bethlehem. When these two arrive Ruth stands apart, an observer, as Naomi is received by God's people. This may be her moment of truth. Would these people of God be the same beautiful, godly people as Naomi was in Ruth's eyes, despite her present pain? True godliness accepts God's people even when they fail. People who leave churches because they are disappointed in the members are guilty of looking in the wrong direction. Jesus never disappoints; keep your eyes on Him.

SECTION VII:
GOD KNOWS YOUR NAME

chapter thirty-six

GOD KNOWS YOUR NAME

Now the two of them went until they came to Bethlehem. And it happened, when they had come to Bethlehem, that all the city was excited because of them; and the women said, "Is this Naomi?"

—Ruth 1:19

Naomi Is Still Known

Naomi and Ruth's arrival sets that holy city abuzz with talk. The talk continues till this very day! The circumstances are all set in the providence of God, to turn human tragedy into human fulfillment. However, if the human dimension is all we see, we miss recognizing the providence of God in salvation. Ruth will be part of that providence, though she knows nothing of it.

We know what that great plan was. It was the plan of God to send His only Son to this world, who, by His suffering, would reconcile us to Himself by the blood shed on the cross of Calvary.

If you are a believer, you too are part of something more than the merely human. You are part of that great eternal work God is doing. Perhaps you do not fully understand it either! Faith calls us to believe for such massive spiritual happenings, even in the midst of interminable pain and deep personal suffering. Lonely Ruth and dejected Naomi will find themselves in the hearts of God's people everywhere for centuries to follow, right into eternity. Ruth tells us to be godly and therefore to take a long-term view of life. Long-term for the Christian…is eternity!

Being Ruth

So Naomi was remembered. What kept her in mind? Was it that she had escaped the famine while they were left to suffer alone? We do not know, but the Bible narrative emphasizes that *"It happened...that all the city was excited because of them"*! What is going on? The phrase seems to suggest that they were glad to see her back home again. Coming back to Bethlehem would be seen by them as the return of a backslider. They left God's people and went to the heathen! That was backsliding then, and it would be backsliding now! Their excitement seems to be a happy excitement, and it may well suggest that they had kept Naomi and her family in their prayers through all of those years. This thought raises the question: What did they pray for them to experience?

Please never think the Lord has forgotten you. He knows your name; He will recognize you instantly; He has been with you all the way. He never left you at all for one moment.

How are we to pray for a backslidden believer? How long are we to keep hoping for their return? How should they be greeted when they do? Many a parent has hoped and prayed daily for such a scenario to occur. Many leadership groups in churches have also equally prayed, perhaps more theologically properly than the laity, maybe less lovingly, less sympathetically, but none the less energetically. Before the throne of God, the vials are emptied out, the vials of the prayers of the saints. All varied, maybe even contradictory. God answers them all accordingly.

The parents would weep tears of gratitude. How would the elders react? The "oversight" of some churches, even today, would call a meeting to discuss possible censure or rehabilitation. The congregation, where the normal human response is generally seen, is more likely to be exactly like these inhabitants of Bethlehem, excited. Overjoyed to see their old friend, their sister in the Lord, home again.

It is arguable that these imagined elders would not be as cold as the illustration suggests. Perhaps just a little cautious initially, but when they heard Naomi's response to all the excitement, they too would express a more measured, hopeful, even joyful, excitement at her return. Their natural concern as natural elders may indeed be very biblical. They are the overseers of the Church of God. They must guard the glory of God and the purity of the church (long-forgotten concepts, perhaps). The conduct and character of the members of the church must be watched over and held in view to ensure that God is glorified in His saints. While many get it all wrong, some get it gloriously right.

Hopefully, upon observing Naomi's humility, they too, like a certain father in the New Testament, would have organized a celebration. To welcome the prodigal back to the fold. Past forgotten, sins forgiven, a new beginning, without recrimination.

chapter thirty-seven

BEING STUCK

But she said to them, "Do not call me Naomi; call me Mara, for the Almighty has dealt very bitterly with me."
—Ruth 1:20

The Scripture gives us the record of Naomi's response to the people. The text says, *"But [Naomi] said…'Do not call me Naomi.'"* These are words to ponder. Hers is an attitude to ponder. This spirit in Naomi calls for us to consider our own response when our decisions go badly wrong.

It is probable that in this part of the narrative you have the unique picture of everybody getting it right. The people welcome her unconditionally. My imagined elders stay quiet for a while. The sinner expresses a beautiful humble spirit that does not run from the censure of the Almighty but accepts it gratefully as a sign of sonship. This prodigal, if this is what Naomi is, is not swept away by the excitement of recognition, but later she will recall it and be comforted.

Naomi holds her ground. Her life circumstances are undeniable. The Almighty has dealt with her bitterly. But she holds the humble position of the believer under apparent censure and takes the chastening of the Lord, which is not pleasant, and quietly submits and waits to see what He will do now. The people hold their breath to see what their gracious God will do to comfort His child, and they give thanks that it was not their own failed enterprises that were exposed! Remember, it was their harvest that failed in the first place.

Did they recognize that failed harvest as the Lord's discipline? Perhaps they recognized that the famine Elimelech fled from was

God chastening them, and they found in their hearts not a judgmental spirit but a common humbled spirit. Also they might have seen the possibility that this recent blessing of a good harvest was God's token of His pleasure and that Naomi's return was a blessing.

The Lord who had visited His people with bread, that Lord, must have been satisfied to see that His plan to bring Ruth to Bethlehem was worked out. He planned it in eternity. Nobody in that day fully understood what God was doing. We are the ones who see it all. *"These all died in faith, not having received the promises,"* as Hebrews says (Hebrews 11:13). We see; we are given the privilege in these last days of seeing it all played out before us, though not in every detail.

Naomi says, "Do not call me Naomi." Her name means "pleasant." She insists that this name must be changed. It no longer fits her. She still feels, even after her long walk home, a peculiar sense of failure. There are some requests that are best forgotten by us. There is no record of her having done anything wrong! The story at the very beginning tells us *"a certain man"* took his family (Ruth 1:1). It is quite possible that Naomi was enthusiastic about this proposal. Then again, she might equally have objected all the way and been as silent on their outgoing journey from Bethlehem to Moab, as she was on this return journey with Ruth!

"The Almighty has dealt very bitterly with me." Bitterly means sorely with an abiding deep-knotted kind of pain. How right she seems to be! How long is it since her husband died? That's not certain in the narrative, but it's not long since her two sons died. Naomi is in the long healing period where grief is a diminishing quiet background reality. To expect too much definition, too much theological correctness, in her repentance might be a little unreasonable. She needs time to heal in heart and head. Then the true nature of her "return" will be visible to all. Be careful of backsliding; the Lord will use all means to bring you back. Gently, at first, but He never gives up. And let Naomi's real discomfort here be a caution to any who imagine a better world outside of God's Church.

Being Stuck

"*Call me Mara*," which means "bitter," says Naomi. This is how Naomi reads the events of her journey to Moab and her return. So sad an assessment of life. How like so many people today! Many read their own lives as such, in the secrecy of their own heart. Life can be really hard, unfair, downright wrong! At least from a human point of view. Some people cannot actually give a reasonable full explanation as why their life is so bad. Often, it is clearly their own fault. They did not take good advice. They acted from bad motives. They gave up at the first difficulty. Many examinations of lives conclude that self is to blame, self in all its negative senses.

Fewer exhibit what we appear to have here—natural unavoidable circumstances going askew in a short time, resulting in ruin, and in a foreign land. We do not know what caused the death of her two sons. One way or the other it was a tragic story of epic proportions for any individual. Nothing was going to bring them back. No amount of sympathy, no amount of company or counsel, will restore her family. Is there help for Naomi?

We love to think that there is always an answer, always help in counsel. The Bible sends such souls to their knees, to cry in the presence of a loving heavenly Father, and there to find not just spiritual comfort but the Holy Spirit Himself. The person of the Holy Spirit. The Paraclete, the one who "draws beside us." Herein lies the unique help of the believer. No man can replace Him. None should risk such blasphemy.

Sometimes we have set ourselves up as better than God, intruding into God's work, to relieve "Naomi" in her anguish. Learn when your limit has been reached. Do not feel helpless; just direct those you cannot comfort to the throne of grace. It is a real place! Only there is real comfort found! In the Church we have given human counsellors too much credence that belongs to Jesus Christ. Have we forgotten it was founded at Pentecost? There in that upper room God's Holy Spirit came to a group of terrified disciples, and that profound experience turned them into men who turned the world upside down! He is still present in His Church at every meeting. He will finish the work in Naomi that He began.

chapter thirty-eight

THE GODLESS ALGORITHM

> *"I went out full, and the Lord has brought me home again empty. Why do you call me Naomi, since the LORD has testified against me, and the Almighty has afflicted me?"*
> —Ruth 1:21

Godly Suffering

When Naomi responds to the townspeople's excitement, she's not confessing sin as such. But she's reading circumstances and seeing them through this kind of thinking. She has put together certain circumstances and produced a pattern that has become a rigid and constant reading of events. This pattern reads like this: Went out full; came back empty. Empty equals failure, equals backsliding, equals God is against me! What a common Christian algorithm! We reduce God's dealings to our own interpretation instead of seeing His dealings in the overall teaching of the Bible, which do not present such a rigid, dismal God.

Yes, there are times when God chastens us, there are times when trouble is entirely our own fault, and occasionally God is dealing with us in correction. But our troubles are not all necessarily our fault; nor are they all necessarily God's chastening. They never declare that God is against us. They certainly do not declare that He has deserted us! We may not have deserved the pain we are in, but God in His wise providence and in the furtherance of His divine plan has allowed trouble to come. Talk to Job!

Naomi in this narrative is blaming God for her husband's death, for the deaths of her two sons. For famines in Bethlehem and famines in Moab. These are cruel accusation against the Almighty. In fact we see that this God is planning an event that will defeat death! On the cross of Calvary, in a day to come. It is this God who gave His people bread (Ruth 1:6) who promised that *"While the earth remains, seedtime and harvest...shall not cease"* (Genesis 8:22). He is a good God.

What a sad view of the Almighty! He is not like us. *"He has not... punished us according to our iniquities"* (Psalm 103:10). Forgiveness is with the Lord (Psalm 130:4). Many a pastor has had to defend God at a hospital bed when a devoted godly believing patient attributes their cancer to God's punishing them for ancient sins of their youth, long since confessed. Forgiven and forgotten by the Almighty, but not by themselves. *"Peace, goodwill toward men"* (Luke 2:13–14) is the gospel promise.

God is working out a great and awesome plan. He will execute it to the letter. He has started it, and He will bring it to a wonderful conclusion. He will be glorified even in the suffering of His saints. Do not minimize the reality that is suffering. It is here to stay for a while yet, until Jesus returns to take us home. Not one day before. Furthermore, that suffering may be serving to bring you closer to the Lord you love, either in your soul or in your life. He is waiting for you at the gate of heaven. He will say, *"Well done, good and faithful servant"* (Matthew 25:21). And you will have a new name, and it will not be "Mara"! There will be nothing to be bitter about then. No need for recriminations or pain. No tears.

The narrative ends this part of the story on this uncertain, rather dissonant, note: *"I went out full, and the LORD has brought me home again empty."* The people may have had their enthusiasm dampened a little by Naomi's miserable insistence. But it all is quietly left behind as the narrative concludes with a brief, ever so concise, new note. The subject of bitterness is soon to be replaced by the subject of barley! Often God's corrective and comforting ministrations take on the form of normal and natural events like a barley harvest.

The writer tells us, "*Now they came to Bethlehem*" (Ruth 1:22). "*They*," not "*the two of them*," as in the early part of the narrative. Now these two are mysteriously one! The writer is inspired to use one word instead of two: "they"! This little insignificant word is the clue to all the blessing to follow. It is the end of all the misery in the book of Ruth. We are about to see who Naomi's irritating companion really was. This Ruth, this meaninglessly named young Moabite woman, who is she? She is, and has been, for all of the time past in this story, God's answer to all of Naomi's problems!

Ruth is like so many in the Scriptures before and after her own time. Just like Joseph, Joash, David, Esther. And what about Jesus Himself? "*He came to His own, and His own did not receive Him*" (John 1:11). This is the company Ruth keeps in the history of salvation. What's barley got to do with it? God loves suspense! It is what faith feeds upon!

SECTION VIII:
BARLEY HARVEST

SECTION FOUR
BARLEY HARVEST

chapter thirty-nine

A NEW BEGINNING

> *So Naomi returned, and Ruth the Moabitess her daughter-in-law with her, who returned from the country of Moab. Now they came to Bethlehem at the beginning of barley harvest.*
> —Ruth 1:22

This verse is a summary of the story so far and an introduction to the next section. We can further abbreviate it to "Naomi...Ruth...harvest"! These three words show the development of the book of Ruth so far. They might well be said to indicate a progression through the first chapter of the book of Ruth: bitterness followed by commitment followed by a journey to fullness.

Naomi's bitterness is set so gently against Ruth's godly commitment. Both rise together to the fullness of God's "barley harvest." God had given His people bread indeed! Both the bitterness of death and the sacrificial pain of commitment will be comforted by the overwhelming love shown in God's abundant harvest.

Strive always to see your own situation as an opportunity for God to reveal Himself. Never shrink into complaining at God or men. Always find God before you look at men. You will see your environment differently if you see it in His presence first.

God certainly sees our emptiness as His opportunity to fill us afresh. He brought you to this place of emptiness like Naomi, even like Ruth. He brought these two women both back to Bethlehem, Judah, empty widows, to fill them with His abundance, a harvest so great that it was talked about in Moab! They heard about it in

Moab, not realizing— how could they realize?— that this visitation from God in Bethlehem was for them.

They arrived at the beginning of barley harvest. The gleaners had so much grain that they left more than normal behind for Ruth to gather. This is the God of the Bible. If you are empty, even bitterly so, God has been preparing for you for a long time. Perhaps in the autumn or the spring before you left your "Moab," God planted some seeds in your "Bethlehem." He intended them to be ready for your moment of need. This is God's care for us, His providence toward us, summed up simply as His foresight and His provision. He sees before the trouble comes, and He makes provision for it in advance.

Naomi and Ruth did not need to see the details. They only needed to see the Lord. Evidence of this new alignment is shown in Naomi rising to go back to Bethlehem, Judah, and in Ruth's vibrant commitment to all that was Naomi. We are to understand that they gave themselves to the Lord at the crossroads in Moab. He gave them a barley harvest.

The reapers were part of this great provision of God for Naomi and Ruth. Notice that what they discard is God's provision. What they ignore, what they leave on the ground as mere "leftovers," God prepared and purposefully takes out of the reapers' hand and places it where Ruth will see it. What a God! What provision! What detail! Notice that God's provision is naturally miraculous. It is real grain, not magically produced out of nothing. It is harvested by others for them; it did not fall out of the sky. While every seed that grows is a miracle of God's creation, here it is not the grain itself that is the miracle; it is the timing of that grain and the coming together of people and places. A harvest is undoubtedly a miraculous event, produced by God. But the farmers have to plant the grain, and Ruth has to pick it up with a sore back. See how in this entire story none of the characters seem to know what God is doing. They are all out of it to some degree. Plenty is always ahead of them.

Oh what a wonderful way the Holy Spirit ends human hopelessness in one word: *harvest*! Naomi, Ruth, are you listening? Did you hear it? In the midst of anguish of soul and defeat at the hands

A New Beginning

of circumstances beyond your control, at the end of your road, a harvest of hope is just suddenly and inexplicably there. God has the last word always! What a God is Jehovah God! What mercy to the empty heart and soul! What beloved kindness, what care, and above all, what divine provision! What providence!

This is the story of—who? Ruth? No, at this point in the story it is more about Naomi. But in the bigger picture, yes, it is all about Ruth, because in the great providence of God in eternity, this young woman was set apart to be a part of the genealogy of Jesus Christ.

chapter forty

A RICH RELATIVE

There was a relative of Naomi's husband, a man of great wealth, of the family of Elimelech. His name was Boaz.
—Ruth 2:1

The story moves on, introducing us here to Boaz, a relative of Elimelech's. The name *Boaz* means "swift strength," a name that sounds like he was prepared at birth to intervene in this needy situation. Naomi and Ruth need a swift solution to their problem. Widows the world over, since time began, have been the downtrodden of every culture. Still today every pastor knows this. Yes, there are wealthy widows also, but the norm for widows is not wealth. In the Western world many are well looked after. But a widow who has fallen on bad times often has nowhere to turn.

Many "widows" in our present world had a husband who left them. The law does its best, but often miserably, to deal with the needs of older women who must live alone for whatever reasons. They can be a very sad and silent group. The New Testament rule was to care for widows who were "*really widows*" (1 Timothy 5:3). Boaz perhaps came to Naomi's mind. Perhaps she had never had any real dealings with him. But God had been dealing with Boaz throughout his entire life, blessing him with good character and good training in life. God had blessed his harvests, especially this most recent one, because God would make Boaz a servant to His will.

Wealthy people must, and often do, realize their moral obligation to help the needy. This is a biblical principle, but it also seems to be part of the human makeup. It does not need laws or government rules; it just requires a soft heart. We do not need definitions laid out by parliaments to define this need. We need conscience, not tax concessions. A conscience kept alive by our own diligence. Here we are dealing with two widows, a double need. They will do all they can to help themselves. However, Boaz is essential to this book. His genealogy runs in the messianic line. And Ruth will bear him a son.

chapter forty-one

THE MOABITE BECOMES MY DAUGHTER

> *So Ruth the Moabitess said to Naomi, "Please let me go to the field, and glean heads of grain after him in whose sight I may find favor." And she said to her, "Go, my daughter."*
>
> —Ruth 2:2

Until this moment, Ruth is still seen as the Moabitess! It is just a shorthand way to explain her away. We already know, but is the writer trying to hint at something? This may well be an indication that these two women, newly arrived in Bethlehem, Judah, are still not one. Naomi has expressed a strange attitude toward Ruth. She has welcomed her into her family as the wife of her son. She has also sent her back to Moab and to her gods! She could not stop her going with her to Bethlehem, But it was despite Naomi, and Naomi is unhappy, even grudging, toward her. Even after Ruth's impassioned commitment to her, she does not seem moved—for example, as moved as we are! She treats her with silence. Is there a more hurtful thing we can do to another human being than refuse to speak? To turn away and not respond? To shut them down?

Ruth is still "the Moabitess" at this point in the narrative. That is what the inspired writer is telling us in the introduction to this part of the story. However, we are hoping that the Lord has worked some change into Naomi on this long walk. The pain of the walk may have to ease before it becomes evident. But something is changing, and it can be seen in this verse. Ruth the Moabitess at the beginning of the verse becomes Ruth *"my daughter"* at the end of the verse! What has happened?

Well, they walked for days. On arrival at Bethlehem there is no comment in the narrative to tell us that conversation had resumed or the relationship had improved. Two things are recorded for us to ponder. One is Naomi's conversation with the people of Bethlehem, Judah. They received her despite her negative, sad response. Yet perhaps their enthusiasm and excitement over her softened her and gave her hope. Then Ruth asked permission to glean. Here are two things that may have worked together to reach dear Naomi in her depths. Did she sleep a few days and rest and pray or just think? Or did the Lord open her heart like Lydia's in the book of Acts? She is different here than she was upon leaving Moab—that seems certain. The long walk also surely made her malleable, easier to be changed. When the narrative records for us that Naomi said, "*Go, my daughter,*" we have a little glimpse of the Naomi we had come to love but seemed to have lost on the journey home. I think she's back with us here!

Ruth's heart must have risen in thanksgiving when she heard these two words. Not just "Go" but "Go, my daughter." Remember, just a few days back in the story, Naomi told Ruth to go back. It was not said in a rejecting or angry way—of course not—but it was said, and it was painful. Now the word "go" is softened by the maternal "my daughter."

Ruth is keen and asks Naomi to allow her to go into the fields and glean. This humility and respect expressed by Ruth toward Naomi is something we could learn from in our dealings between age groups today. It may have been the final key to unlock Naomi from her stubborn, sullen silence. It may have caused her to see differently and recognize her own miserable demeanour. We should try this giving of respect to the older person, recognizing them, acknowledging them as special for their years. This moment of dignity may have encouraged Naomi, may have released these two beautiful words "my daughter" and reset a whole relationship.

Ruth goes to "*glean... after him in whose sight I find favor.*" Note that this is essentially all Ruth needs, someone to be kind. Just an open, free spirit. Often such an insignificant look in an eye of a passerby in a church can make a person open up to listen to the good news.

Ruth is a foreigner! Nobody needs to feel any particular call to help her. Charity begins at home, and there are poor Israelites. Yet all it will take is one reaper to recognize a human being and lay aside national and cultural, yes, and even religious prejudice and smile. No need to talk; just look at her—your face will tell all! But be careful, because had they known who she was, they would have given her all she wanted and more, instantly!

Israel had teaching on how to treat foreigners and strangers. They themselves had been strangers in a foreign land. Someone smiled at Ruth. Someone's eye lit up enough to let her feel comfortable. Was that too hard? Was it a great effort? No, it was not, but it was necessary and beautiful. The unspoken acknowledgement of her presence as being acceptable must have warmed her heart. Now she must have felt good to be there. Ruth the foreigner found favour among a particular group of reapers.

chapter forty-two

GLEANING

The practice of gleaning was established in Israel early. It was the practice of not harvesting every single part of the crop. Allowance was made for areas of the field to be left for the poor to gather. Reapers were not to pick up every piece of grain they accidentally dropped. if they missed some, they were not to return for it. This was a social welfare system in ancient Israel.

Interestingly, access was not restricted to poor Israelis. Any poor person could glean this leftover harvest. On the other hand, it was not entirely a free giveaway. The poor or even the elderly had to go and glean themselves. There was no social structure organized by governments. There was no government oversight or policing of this. Conscience was its master and monitor. And it worked for centuries! The idea was used outside of Israel in other agricultural societies and communities. Ruth, with Naomi's blessing, eagerly went to glean with the poor.

The Lord sometimes reduces us to poverty to teach us or to test us. He knows the real benefit that can be gained from a short experience of poverty—only if it is responded to properly, of course. However, the Bible never elevates poverty itself to being a virtue. We all know that in small doses it can be very beneficial in teaching us to be humble and to appreciate little things, to reset our priorities and values. Poverty for a time may not be that bad! We may even come to value it for the lessons we learn there. We may never view the poor the same again. We may also have bigger hearts and smaller eyes.

Note that our Saviour was born into relative poverty and spoke and ministered to the poor. Remembering the poor was a standard practice in the New Testament Church. In the Western world, we seem to find it hard to identify true poverty. We spend lots of time and money trying to help those who will not be helped, those we might describe as not *"widows who are really widows"* (1 Timothy 5:3), ashamed to work, unwilling to take the menial or necessary course of action, but expecting others to go the extra mile to reach them in their chosen comfort zone, be it drugs or drink or destitution of any sort.

The gospel does not send the Church corporate to fix these things. The "Church" as an institution or as an organism has a mandate to make disciples, and everything is subordinate to that. Social enterprise has been the ruin of many churches. But we must acknowledge that God teaches us to look out for the genuine and real poor. As believers we are not at liberty to ignore what is in front of us in terms of real needs. We cannot pass it on to our brother, let alone to the whole Church. It used to be said, "If you get the vision, you fulfill it"! Much truth is there, and much error is exposed by the pithy little saying.

Here some overlooked grain is appreciated by Ruth. God often causes things to "spill out" for the good of the one in need. Just a few pieces of grain from a full harvest, but the beginning of a new life for Ruth and for Naomi. So here we have Naomi and Ruth sitting in the place they have found to live and talking about their future. At a very basic level, finding food!

We have just read that Boaz was a very wealthy man. Why did the Lord not just instantly connect them? God seldom does one thing without touching lots of others in the process. *"My ways [are] are higher than your ways, and My thoughts than your thoughts"* (Isaiah 55:8–9). Ruth is apparently keen to get to work! What a blessing to have such a spirit. Here, this spirit is not just produced by necessity. This diligence in Ruth is character based, as is seen from her sense of commitment to Naomi. Ruth has been taught well and raised well—yes, even in Moab! Her belief set had to be given to her by Elimelech, Naomi and Mahlon.

Christians can have the strangest notions about non-Christians, especially the children of Christian homes who have lived their lives in the church culture of their day. They can get all askew in their thinking about the "world." Christians are not the only people who can have high standards of behaviour. It's not difficult to recognize the benefits of good behaviour. Even atheists want people to be kind. This is the image of God in every man. We do well to let it shine even if we do not believe in Him, because to ignore its influence is to produce a world without standards of any kind. Many heathen people have high standards of behaviour. Often it is limited in its scope of activity, but where care is recognized and where basic human inclinations are allowed to be encouraged, they can produce happy societies. Not perfect societies, certainly not godly societies, and sin generally is their downfall despite the image of God and their attempts to produce just cultures.

> *Then she left, and went and gleaned in the field after the reapers. And she happened to come to the part of the field belonging to Boaz, who was of the family of Elimelech.*
> —Ruth 2:3

A simple observation will note that the Ruth, who will never leave Naomi, cheerfully leaves her! The full wholehearted commitment Ruth made was a balanced and sensible thing, not an obsessive grasping at something. Then she *"happened to come to the part of the field belonging to Boaz."* She had no idea who Boaz was, let alone where his field started and another man's stopped. The fields were often marked by stones or geographical changes. The fields were all one big field, but the reapers know where their field started and finished. They may have been hired to work in more than one field. Often if a land owner had a lot of land he would have his own hired reapers, and they would only work his land. This seems to have been the case with Boaz.

So quickly this story of tragedy and death has moved away from misery. Quite suddenly it has become a pastoral harvest story.

The atmosphere of the story, the character of the language, is becoming industrious, even positive and upbeat, but not yet cheerful. The story is in character with harvest and all that season carried. But it has all happened so quickly. We have moved on without perhaps realizing it.

As if by accident, Ruth comes to the field belonging to Boaz. Note in this part of the book of Ruth how many such "chance happenings" occur. They do not occur by chance…they are clearly and undeniably workings of the providences of God! Watch for them. When they occur in your life, acknowledge them publicly!

SECTION IX:
BEING EXAMINED

chapter forty-three

WHOSE YOUNG WOMAN IS THIS?

Now behold, Boaz came from Bethlehem, and said to the reapers, "The LORD be with you!" And they answered him, "The LORD bless you!"

—Ruth 2:4

The field was some distance from Bethlehem, a distance worth mentioning because it required some organization to visit it. It was not a daily event! Ruth walked to the field, but that is what poor people have to do. Boaz, on the other hand, would visit different fields at different times. The Bible says, *"Now behold, Boaz came."* What is the surprise element it wants us to notice? Surely it is that this was a remarkable providence! Boaz came on the very day Ruth had begun to work in a randomly chosen field. If that reaper had not smiled, perhaps Ruth would have moved to another field. Never discount the usefulness of a simple kindness.

Boaz conveys a godly blessing on his workers: *"The LORD be with you!"* This is our introduction to the man Boaz. First impressions are at least interesting. In this case Boaz is seen to be a man who acknowledges God in his daily life. In his working life! He does so openly before his workforce. Boaz is a wise man; he speaks to his workforce; he communicates. He is a spiritual man. He is not ashamed of what he believes or of the God in whom he trusts.

"And they answered him, 'The LORD bless you!'" They also freely communicate with Boaz, and in similar godly terms. This seems like a civilized working environment. It has a happy ring to it in this good year of harvest. But it must have been set in place

during the earlier bad years as well. Bless the Lord in the good years. Also do so in the years of famine. Praise must be consistent to be meaningful. It is the *"song as in the night"* (Isaiah 30:29), the *"at midnight...singing hymns to God"* (Acts 16:25) in the prison, that raises the notice of the world around us. They understand how hard it is to do that.

> *Then Boaz said to his servant who was in charge of the reapers, "Whose young woman is this?"*
> —Ruth 2:5

What was the concern here? Boaz recognized that Ruth was new. He showed an interest in people even down there at the level of the poor folk following the reapers. But he had no real idea who it was that he was asking about. God only knew what the future held for these two souls! See God bringing the greatest into contact with the least, as if by chance, yet not by chance. Men who do not believe in God declare famines as His failures! Unbelief only ever acknowledges God in famine, never in plenty. Believers acknowledge God in both good and bad, by faith, even when He is hidden.

We instantly like Boaz. His name has a pleasant ring to it. But it is the little conversational pieces that enable us to recognize someone we might just like. He sounds like a friendly boss. The Bible, Old and New Testaments, expects the believers to carry themselves in a particular way, whatever their position, in such a way as to bring glory to God from the onlookers and to bring some satisfaction out of a working day for the workers and for the owners. Not just in monetary terms; money is not all there is to any day. We do well to establish what we want out of a day early in life. Better if possible to determine what we will contribute to a day first. Both Ruth and Boaz have set this day apart distinctly in their minds for a good purpose—Ruth to feed Naomi, and Boaz to encourage his workforce, from the head reaper to the newest and lowest class of workers in his field.

Whose Young Woman Is This?

So the servant who was in charge of the reapers answered and said, "It is the young Moabite woman who came back with Naomi from the country of Moab."

—Ruth 2:6

This indicates that Ruth and her coming from Moab were widely known. Her story was now perhaps common knowledge. Boaz may have heard of her but it appears had never seen her until now. Ruth had made an impression on a whole community, a whole city. Ruth herself was probably unaware of this. Often we are the last people to understand the effect of our actions. So we should have more faith and believe that when we ask the Lord at the beginning of each day to make us a blessing to someone, He actually will, and then look for such a response over the day in order to return thanks in the evening.

Boaz had a head reaper who took the same interest in his workers as his boss Boaz did. Good or bad often filters down through the ranks. Here we have that good sense of a caring environment bouncing back up again, right to Boaz. Would it not be a good intention to let people know you are who you are because of Jesus? Use your imagination to tell them. Because you really are where you are because He made you a certain kind of person; He never left you to the random tides and currents of life. He is your guide and comforter.

"And she said, 'Please let me glean and gather after the reapers among the sheaves.' So she came and has continued from morning until now, though she rested a little in the house."

—Ruth 2:7

The servant relates Ruth's request to glean after the reapers. He shows her diligence over the whole day. She worked hard enough to need to rest, but she rested only a little! Not because she did not need more rest but because she needed food more than rest. Ruth was certainly not lazy!

Being Ruth

If ever we want to see how beautiful a connection there is between hard work and joyfulness, go to a farm at harvest time. So much of the real beauty has been removed by machinery, but the atmosphere is still there. That short journey from the field to the barn on the cart loaded with the crop, the sun setting, and workers singing all the way back and forth is a memory to be relished. Filling up the barn until you are squeezing and pushing bales of hay into the high places of the loft space, then gathering round a fire or a kitchen table with food and fellowship...there are few more wholesome and happy places.

Even though we live under the curse of Eden, God has poured out his mercy on sinners and given, given, given. He has showered us with good things. In such a happy environment, God is working! Here in the book of Ruth, He plans another harvest. A harvest of souls redeemed by precious blood shed on Calvary's cross. Still to come, but including these very people in this story. See how the gospel weaves through the affairs of men! Boaz has been introduced to us; now he will be introduced to Ruth.

chapter forty-four
BEING A LISTENER

> *Then Boaz said to Ruth, "You will listen, my daughter, will you not? Do not go to glean in another field, nor go from here, but stay close by my young women."*
>
> —Ruth 2:8

Boaz's conversation with Ruth is an appeal. They have only just met. Language reveals so much. With few words it creates pictures and images. In seconds words bare the heart of the speaker, for better or worse. Boaz makes an appeal to Ruth before he makes his points. He says, "*You will listen, my daughter.*" This is not unique speech. It is speech we all recognize. It is a gentle command expecting a good response. The command is supported by an affectionate warmth, suggesting a command for our protection.

He calls her "*my daughter.*" He is no doubt older than her, perhaps even significantly older than her. The command is then backed by a rhetorical question. He asks, "*Will you not?*" But the answer is assumed to be agreeable. It is not a threat but more an affirmation of her character. Boaz has learned about Ruth and can reasonably expect a response based on good sense.

Sometimes the Lord speaks to us like this. Sometimes we need commands; sometimes we need veiled threats. Occasionally we even need to be warned! However, be it threats, veiled or unveiled, or warnings, the expectation of the speaker is that the threat will never be enacted because obedience is fully expected! Obedience is assumed, even if only on the basis of fear, but never cringing fear.

The language of threats, in the Bible, is to be measured against the expectation of a good response.

Ruth is given the option to refuse or to listen carelessly, but Boaz confirms her as his "daughter" by putting words in her mouth that respond positively to his appeal. He gives the warning to sharpen her attention, while assuring her of an expectation that reveals a close relationship. The book of Hebrews, often misunderstood, uses similar language of warning to reinforce and confirm the Hebrew believers. It is the language of parental care to the believing child of God.

"*Do not go to glean in another field.*" Here Boaz strengthens her expected agreement. He does this by filling out her understanding of the practical implications of "listening." This will ensure a total harmonizing of purpose between the two.

Good preaching does this in accordance with the passage being taught. The Scriptures must be applied to daily life. Often preaching is aimed totally at problem solving or comfort giving. Often, even the good expository preacher restrains himself from application. Application can be seen as the grubby end of preaching. It can be viewed as ranting, and it indeed can fall into all the dangers and pitfalls of every other aspect of the art. Some preachers love it, and some fill out their lack of study or understanding by extending the legitimate proportions measured between teaching and preaching and application. But the good preacher understands the human heart and knows like Boaz did that even the most gentle determined follower of Jesus Christ needs a "spur" to obedience now and again, however brief, however strong.

Boaz strikes a healthy balance here, providing Ruth with a warm-hearted exhortation strengthened by an expectation of obedience and just a hint of warning. The good preacher must spell out the practical implications and blessings of obedience but must also then at least give a measured moment to the implications and dangers associated with disobedience.

Boaz defines obedience here: "*Do not go to glean in another field.*" Every preacher or teacher, every parent or counsellor, should aspire to be thorough. Boaz is not just repeating the same message over and over again. He is spelling out what is meant by his initial guarded message: "*You will listen...will you not?*" That means, says Boaz, "*Do not go to glean in another field.*" It also means, more basically, do not go from here.

Some believers have left their church on Sunday and practised the very opposite of what they were taught from God's Word in the sermon. Many more have not been so blatant in their disobedience but disobeyed nevertheless. They simply did not do what they were commanded, even when their obedience was gently requested. Both equally fail in their response to God's Word. Here Boaz, understanding the nature of a failure to comply, adds this warning: "*Do not...go from here*"! Yes, Ruth may have gone to the neighbouring field and gleaned all day. On the other hand, she may simply have gone home to Naomi for coffee! Both actions are disobedient.

Some churches choose to analyze failure by degrees. This has a place among men, but in the eyes of God both here are disobedience, plain and simple. Boaz knows the propensity of sin to ease its way into a situation. Ruth is not likely to leave Boaz's field., but she may be tempted to simply go to the next field for a casual gleaning. Boaz knows this could remove her from a safety net that he could not provide in any field.

He goes even further in giving good advice. He says, "*Stay close by my young women.*" In this statement Boaz is providing a safety net for Ruth that he knows she will need. She may not know what dangers are present for a woman among a field of reapers. Why should she stay among the young women? Why remain close by their side, a "conversational" distance, we might say? Because the young men have already been making their predictable advances to Boaz's younger women. These women know what to expect and from whom, which of the young men are honourable and which are not.

Note that Ruth is not a teenager here but maybe thirty-something years old. She had been married for ten years. The other women would quite likely be much younger, even by more than ten years. Sometimes, surprisingly, this can be an area where the younger can instruct the older. They can do this from real experience that is absolutely up to date. Though there is nothing new in human relations, it seems that every new generation has to learn all the subtitles and innuendoes and how to distinguish between the serious and the frivolous and develop a sense for the downright evil, without any need for detailed education! What a help to us is the image of God, which is stamped on every man! Beware of those in whom that image has been obliterated by wickedness.

When a more mature woman returns to the realm of "singleness," she is very vulnerable. She may not be naive, but she may have lost that instant sense of self-preservation that is thankfully, and often, common in youth. Younger women have a natural and learned sense of self-protection. They have something specific to lose. The experienced woman may not have that fear of loss. She may have lots of other fears associated with men but in fact may be attracted where she should be running away! Boaz is protecting Ruth where women are undoubtedly in a measure of danger, among a group of young working men. Some things will never change!

Another reason this is good advice is because Ruth is a foreigner. This is again another category of vulnerability. A man intent on brute passions needs an intense sense of restraint, often physical restraint. That sense of restraint can be heightened by being in a familiar setting. Take that man out of his home and familiar surroundings and put him among a culture he considers less than his own, and his sense of freedom can be quickly distorted. A foreigner can raise this same sense of disadvantage in the wrong man, or the man who is just basically "wrong"! Boaz knows all of this. All of the ancient societies knew this as a normal understanding of what it was to be foreign.

See the men of Sodom, in Genesis 19. They demand of Lot that he send out the two men who visited him. The men of Sodom, old and young, take offence at Lot for judging them instantly noting that Lot *"came in"* to Sodom (Genesis 19:9). That is, Lot, as well as his guests, was a foreigner to Sodom. They can disregard Lot's judgment and disregard the two men utterly on this simple fact. They think they can treat them any way they choose just because they are all foreign! Nothing has changed; it is only restrained in countries where laws are strongly applied. Boaz is not naive, that is certain. He has been in this business for a while and knows the problems and the dangers associated. He will ensure that Ruth is safe. She will be, so long as she "listens" and acts accordingly.

So will we be safe, if we hear these words of wisdom: Do not leave the fold of God's people unless essential. Stay there; it is the safest place, even though dangers still exist when churches are careless. These days it is imperative that the members of churches hear Boaz's advice to Ruth and employ it. Previous generations were much more careful than we are today. There was less reliance on laws and much more reliance on common understandings about human nature. No need for rules and definitions and safety nets. Parents were the first line of "safety nets." Every church member had antenna that bristled when danger approached.

Niceness is absolutely counterproductive in this discussion. Defence that is instantly willing to be expressed and acted upon is the only and initial way to deal with it. Lot was trying to be nice to the men of Sodom—what a moral travesty he proposed (Genesis 19:6–8).

What a blessing Boaz is being to Ruth when he says, "*Stay close by my young women*"! But Boaz is not finished giving counsel to Ruth about how to live among the reapers! Surely as believers read these words we hear the Lord speaking to us. Jesus says, "*Take My yoke*" (Matthew 11:29); "stay by Me" is the sense. He says, "*My sheep hear my voice, and I know them, and they follow Me*" (John 10:27). Again in this context, "*They will by no means follow a stranger, but will flee from him, for they do not know the voice of strangers*" (John 10:5).

chapter forty-five

BEING FOCUSED

"Let your eyes be on the field which they reap, and go after them. Have I not commanded the young men not to touch you? And when you are thirsty, go to the vessels and drink from what the young men have drawn."
—Ruth 2:9

Boaz says to keep *"your eyes...on the field which they reap."* Keep your eyes on the field! Don't let your gaze wander from the task you are engaged in. Stay focused! Do not slip into casual looking at what's around. Why? Because you might see something attractive!

Sin is not always ugly. It may be attractive and desirable, yet it always remains extremely harmful! Don't look around too much. Stay with what God has given you and what God has given you to do. A moment is all it takes. Eyes reach each other faster than light can supply clear definition and much faster than our brain can make an assessment. An impression is all it takes. Temptation needs no detail. Minimal, vague, no time to think, fast, in a moment is how the devil works. He does not spell it all out for you to examine. He gives the briefest of glances. Just one of these can ruin a whole life.

One glance, and the great King David fell. Because he saw! David took his eyes off his role as commander of the Lord's armies to relax. Instead of surveying the battlefield where his men were, he surveyed the night, perhaps innocently. What did he expect to see? Stars, probably. But his eyes should have been on the battlefield.

He is not in fighting mode tonight, feels no need of armour or weaponry. He's safe, is he? We are never safe in indolence, though it may feel neutral. Nonetheless, he is awake. Perhaps curious. His heart and mind poised in what seems like a balance but is more like the pendulum poised at its extremity. Responsive to any gravitational pull. Poised for a moment and thus free to swing. Swing it did for David!

Men seldom keep balance in anything for long. David's eyes are on Pleiades or Orion or the Great Bear. From the clear distinction of starry galaxies, a momentary mental eclipse, and another magnetism pulls him into a black hole of temptation. A beautiful spectacle bathes! Observation can become temptation instantly.

Just one hazy look is all it took. And therefore Boaz warns us, long before David fell, "Keep your eyes on the field!" Boaz is a good man. Wise and experienced. Spirituality is not naive. His feet are grounded in a real but muddy world. Let us all "listen...will you not?"

He tells Ruth to keep her eyes upon his field. He tells her to follow the right people. I like this man Boaz, don't you? Would you not want him to counsel your daughter? Would you not listen to him yourself? Perhaps there are readers who wish they had had him as their father or a friend, a pastor or a Sunday school teacher. Boaz is grounded in real spirituality. True spirituality is never naive or easily led astray. Reality and spirituality is a powerful combination. *"Stay close by my young women,"* says Boaz (Ruth 2:8). Could it be that he had seen them tried and found faithful? Had he not seen the young men make their approaches and watched their response and felt satisfied? Boaz had a confidence that speaks from observation of these young women, his young women, Ruth's companions-to-be.

The standard in Boaz's field was higher than in other fields. The Church's standards need to be likewise higher, different, safer, more honourable than the world's, not just for the safety of our young women but for the glory of our God among the heathen! Away with trying to be the same as the world—it does not work!

chapter forty-six

BEING YOUNG MEN

> "*Let your eyes be on the field which they reap, and go after them. Have I not commanded the young men not to touch you? And when you are thirsty, go to the vessels and drink from what the young men have drawn.*"
> —Ruth 2:9

Boaz is not putting all the responsibility on Ruth to keep her from temptation.

Boaz has commanded the young men not to touch her! Ruth's command was veiled, gentle. The young men are also commanded, but it is blunt and to the point, like a warning sign: DO NOT TOUCH! This shows a clear understanding of the differences between the two groups. Understanding affects the application of the commands. The same command might apply, but it must be applied differently. We are fast losing such wisdom in our world of fake equality. And we wonder why we are in a mess! Here the Bible sets a standards of behaviour for young men. They have not to touch. They do have to provide water for her. So the message is not to be takers but to be givers. Not to use but to respect. Good advice for us today!

What has thirst got to do with it? Thirst breaks the concentration of diligence. Boaz instructed the young men to draw water. God has provided water for our thirst. Go to it and take of it. There is no need to go anywhere else. Anything that takes your heart or mind away from the things of God is a potential weakness. When your soul gets thirsty, that is when the deep needs of your heart must be met. Go to the supply God has provided, and there quench your thirst. Do not go to the world; go to God's Word.

Here, perhaps at a push for the Bible interpreter, we have a case for young men to be providing the water of the Word for thirsty souls. They should be exercising themselves in the effort of drawing the water of life from God's Holy Word to feed the thirsty so that they will not be tempted away to have their thirst met at the cisterns that can hold no water, the broken cisterns spoken of by the prophet Jeremiah. He said, *"For My people have committed two evils: They have forsaken Me, the fountain of living waters, And hewn themselves cisterns—broken cisterns that can hold no water"* (Jeremiah 2:13).

So Boaz shows himself to be a thorough individual. He understands the nature of sin and knows how to deal with it. He gives Ruth excellent advice. We should listen to him. Ruth does!

chapter forty-seven
BEING GRATEFUL

> *So she fell on her face, bowed down to the ground, and said to him, "Why have I found favor in your eyes, that you should take notice of me, since I am a foreigner?"*
>
> —Ruth 2:10

Not only does Ruth listen to Boaz, she obeys fully. Then she goes another distance, which many of us need to learn. She expresses gratitude. She shows appreciation for his faithful advice and help. She demonstrates physically by falling on her face and bowing to the ground! This is true gratitude. It is not subservient, self-effacing submission. It is genuine heartfelt gratitude. Ruth understands how kind Boaz is being in welcoming her and standing by her. What an example for any legitimate and needy immigrant coming to the Western world today, an example of how to receive and how to be received! Ruth is grateful and expresses it by compliance, humility, and hard work.

She's not just thanking him for good advice. She's amazed that he would take the trouble to notice her! Remember, Naomi told her to go back to Moab. She refused to speak to her on the journey to Bethlehem, Judah. And while there seems to be a closer relationship even in these early days after their arrival, perhaps Ruth is really needing some acceptance, some affirmation of her as a person. For a while before leaving Moab and certainly since she left, she's just been a foreigner, a widow, even a daughter-in-law. These words each can take on a "less than perfect" suggestion if used with innuendo or sarcasm. They can be used to slight a person, to reduce them, even to justify disregard to the extent of abuse. Many names used for immigrants are dehumanizing. Boaz, like Naomi, has called her "my daughter"! Now that is human, and it's close and affectionate in a wholesome and safe way.

Ruth fell on her face and said, "Why are you helping me?" Ruth cannot see what there is in herself to warrant Boaz's help, not even enough attraction to cause him to "take notice" of her. Here again is the insecurity, the reduction, of a person who is a widow. This, says Ruth, is doubly amazing since she is a "foreigner"! Ruth knows all the problems associated therewith. She was married to a foreigner for over ten years in Moab. One might think that after a decade you were no longer a foreigner. But she knows you are never very far away from feeling like a foreigner in your own head, sometimes in your own heart as well. Perhaps in the eyes of everyone else too, depending upon many factors outside your control. Boaz is a priceless blessing to someone in Ruth's situation. And yet he cannot fully appreciate just how much of a blessing he is.

However, please note that Boaz is not naive. He did his homework before his kindness to Ruth was expressed. His natural pity for a woman was curtailed in favour of thorough research. His first priority was to his own countrymen; his first duty was to protect them—a lesson we need to learn today, if it is not too late! Boaz was kind only after he had discovered the details about Ruth.

Ruth herself is shocked and amazed by his kindness. She's a complete stranger from another nation. She asks as though there was no reason that would support this action, *"Why have I found favor in your eyes?"*

Boaz replies.

And Boaz answered and said to her, "It has been fully reported to me, all that you have done for your mother-in-law since the death of your husband, and how you have left your father and your mother and the land of your birth, and have come to a people whom you did not know before. The LORD repay your work, and a full reward be

Being Grateful

given you by the LORD God of Israel, under whose wings you have come for refuge."

—Ruth 2:11–12

These two verses give an account of the reasons why Boaz was inclined to help Ruth. His initial human sympathy for her had to be restrained until better reasons than nice feelings appeared. What can we learn from what he says?

First, note that he had an answer! He does not express surprise at the question. He does not express fellow feelings or pity. He does not try to capitalize on the situation for personal gain. He says the reasons are based on a report. He says effectively that he checked up on her! He tells her it was a full report. *"All that you have done,"* he says, has been reported to me. Anything less would be a failure to do due diligence, resulting in more pain for Ruth and Naomi. Boaz would also have some explaining to do to his community, perhaps an explanation like what was demanded from Rahab by the city officials, regarding two foreigners who entered Jericho (Joshua 2)! Ruth does not complain about Boaz checking up on her. She has nothing to hide. And she knows she has no grounds upon which to complain. He, on the other hand, has every right to check up on her.

When Ruth left Moab, she left behind all her rights as a citizen, because that was the only place where she had earned the right to have any rights at all. If Boaz did not accept her, she would have to go back there. That would all fall on her, and certainly not on Boaz or Naomi. Naomi has told what Ruth had done. Naomi acknowledged that all Ruth had done was good. This is perhaps a softening in Naomi since her long walk home. Now it was all recognized as good.

But what Boaz says in verse 12 is also interesting as a report he had about Ruth. He says, *"The LORD repay your work, and a full reward be given you by the LORD God of Israel, under whose wings you have come for refuge."* Here Ruth's kindness to Naomi is seen in the light of a relationship with the God of Israel. Our good work must be done as to the Lord. It must be so identified as to involve the Lord. If we get the praise for our good works, we have robbed God! This is because if it was not for the good work He has done in us through Christ, we would never have done good works. He must be identified as the source of all of our good works.

Ruth is transparent. She's not ashamed. She has accepted the God of Israel as the only true God. In this process of thinking and acting she has rejected all her other gods. And her public testimony has come to be that "under His wings she has come to trust"!

How do we explain our good deeds? Being humble and self-effacing can be admirable, but not if the end result is praise being heaped upon us. We must learn to be brave and bring the Lord into our good works. We must learn to express the gospel freely and clearly with confidence. If we fail to do this, we bring a condemnation on all we have done before God.

Also, look at what trusting in the God of Israel did for Ruth. He brought her out of famine into a land of plenty and is about to restore to her all she lost and more.

Here we also have evidence of a thorough integration into the host nation's culture, religion, work practices, and family standards. Ruth is no longer a Moabitess; she is a believer in the God of Israel. This instantly brings her in line with the culture of Bethlehem, Judah. A refusal to do this would raise questions about what her interests are in the host country. It raises the question of what her influence will be in the host country. It raises the question as to why she ever left her own country if she was not prepared to leave it behind!

Many people forget that the Western world was once brutally uncivilized, as are many countries that people are fleeing from today. But the people fought and died to fix their countries and won at great cost. This fight is what laid the foundation of the great Western nations. They are built upon lives given in the cause of nation building. Many today are not prepared to sacrifice. They prefer an easier route to civilization. It is doubtful still whether they will enjoy civilization or destroy it.

From the narrative it appears that Ruth's case for leaving Moab was an admiration for Naomi and a love for Naomi's God, both of which aided her integration into that society.

chapter forty-eight

BEING COMFORTED

Then she said, "Let me find favor in your sight, my lord; for you have comforted me, and have spoken kindly to your maidservant, though I am not like one of your maidservants."

—Ruth 2:13

Boaz has comforted Ruth. She knows this and appreciates it, like we all do when someone comforts us. Comfort is a very endearing subject in the Bible. It is seen in the Old Testament as something that God longs to give to His people. Hear Isaiah the Prophet: "'*Comfort, yes, comfort My people!' Says your God. 'Speak comfort to Jerusalem'*" (Isaiah 40:1–2). The psalms give thanks for comfort (Psalm 119:49–52).

God wants His people to be able to comfort the afflicted. We might ask ourselves, "When was the last time I comforted someone in trouble?" It is a fundamental characteristic of the Holy Spirit. The Greek word *paraclete* means "one who comes alongside." It is translated in the New Testament as "Comforter." Jesus promised to send Him to do just this for the disciples. He came, and He is still comforting God's people. Affliction leaves us out of sorts, unsettled, indeed not comfortable. We need that infusion often, that saturation, that filling with God's comfort that the Holy Spirit gives. Comfort is not merely a nice feeling; it is an awesome God-given quality. A comfortable person is a substantial person.

Comfort, for Ruth, is very near! But it is in an unexpected place. So many times in the Bible this is the case. God's answer is often among us! Right beside us, like Boaz was for Ruth. And Ruth was for Naomi! Like Jesus was in the boat in the storm with His disciples. When looking for comfort we can be too quick to run to distant places to find it. God is closer than we realize. Look right beside you when you're upset. Try a parent, a sibling, a grandparent, or a pastor or elder before you go running to the internet or a professional stranger!

Right at this moment in the field where Ruth is, she can't speak to Naomi. The Lord knows this and has provided a comforter in Boaz. Right now she's becoming acquainted with him, not realizing the enormous divine industry that has been working to deliver this comfort to her right when she needs it.

God is never stingy with comfort. However, He does responds quicker when active, believing faith is visible. Hear the disappointment in Jesus's words: "*O you of little faith*" (Matthew 8:26). Often God surprises us with the provision He sends to comfort our hearts or minds. God grant that we might also aspire to be His comfort for some needy, afflicted soul today, that we might be a Boaz to some worthy foreigner.

We must comfort "*with the comfort with which we ourselves are comforted by God*" (2 Corinthians 1:4). The Bible uses these words in a spiritual sense. The spiritual sense may limit the application, but it expands the experience. We offer spiritual comfort—that is, comfort from God. This comfort comes with terms of reference. The effect of spiritual comfort can look very like the same comfort the world knows. Spiritual comfort, however, has its source in God and in His Son Jesus Christ.

The rationale of God's comfort is the comfort of a right relationship with Him. The primary focus of God's comfort is His Son, who has made it possible for this relationship to be accomplished. Many believers today are offering spiritual comfort to nonbelievers, and God cannot honour it. His comfort is reserved for His children. This is not black and white; there are lots of exceptions; but as a guide for believers it is essential to understand. Often God allows pain to continue uneased until the pain brings us, believer or unbeliever, to our knees and turns our wayward hearts Godward. Then mercy and love are poured out, and comfort controls the soul. Even when circumstances do not change, or even worsen, we have the greatest of all realized comforts, the assurance that God is in control. When this comfort is ruling in our hearts, we are the most willing of servants.

See Ruth's response to Boaz, and make it your own to the Lord. She submits herself to him, calling herself his *"maidservant."* She also concludes by acknowledging further, *"though I am not like one of your maidservants."* What does she mean? Probably different facial features. Maybe she is older than the others. Dresses differently, poorer even! The differences were probably quite marked, and Ruth felt this keenly. Though she cannot be as one of Boaz's servants, she will become his "maidservant."

> *Now Boaz said to her at mealtime, "Come here, and eat of the bread, and dip your piece of bread in the vinegar." So she sat beside the reapers, and he passed parched grain to her; and she ate and was satisfied, and kept some back.*
> —Ruth 2:14

So many passages of the Old Testament seem to remind us of the Lord's table in the New Testament. There Jesus invites all of us who have received the comfort of saving grace, of salvation delivered, to eat with Him until we are satisfied, and to do this often.

The highest heights and the greatest qualities human ability can reach have all been exhausted in extolling this simple act of eating and drinking. The simplest of souls have given utmost praise from their grateful hearts. All, every single one of them, have laid out their exaltation of this moment. All have failed; all acknowledge this; all recognize the need for such extremes of expression of passion. But all acknowledge the supreme simplicity of the moment when Jesus said, *"Take, eat; this is My body which is broken for you"* (1 Corinthians 11:24).

Being Ruth

We call it by all sorts of religious and sacred names. It is the Lord's Supper, the Table of the Lord, the Sacraments, the Body and the Blood, the Pascal Lamb. Yet it was just a Passover meal of simple bread and simple wine. Just like here in the book of Ruth. Boaz passed parched grain to Ruth. She ate and was sustained. And so too for the believer at the Lord's table. Ruth makes friends and companions at this table, and so do we at the Lord's table. All overseen by Boaz; all overseen by the Lord.

Boaz invites Ruth to sit beside the reapers. At this table all are equal; reapers and gleaners sit together. Jesus invites us to sit beside our brother and sister in Christ, God's people, and be one with them.

Ruth ate, and she *"kept some back."* When she left this precious table, she had something to give! She had more at the end than at the beginning. Something over and above her own needs stayed with her, and it spilled over to Naomi. Believers who have sat with Jesus at His table and partaken of this divine meal should find within themselves a surplus, which must be given away. The Lord's table should take us often, like Ruth in the narrative, directly to the needy! She goes to Naomi. If we ourselves leave that table still hungry in our souls, still not complete, then perhaps something needs attention, and that before we sit with Naomi—certainly before we sit at the Lord's table again!

Look for the grains left over. Look for the divine carelessness illustrated in the reapers leaving grain, dropping grain, making sure the needy, the poor, will find them. God pours out His fullness at this table and encourages us, perhaps commands us, to look for excess and "keep it back" for the poor. Not far from every one of us is a needy soul like Naomi who is still hungry for the Lord.

The Lord's table should not leave us exhausted in any way at all. If you are not full, stay a little longer until you are. If you are full, still stay a little longer. Not to gorge your own soul, even with worship or adoration, but to hold the bread, to preserve some wine, figuratively. Let it mature in your hands and hearts. Then go and find a lost sheep or a hungry heart, a widow or a foreigner. Having satisfied your own soul, keep some back for "Naomi"!

SECTION X:
BEING PROVIDED FOR

chapter forty-nine

GLEANING AMONG THE SHEAVES

And when she rose up to glean, Boaz commanded his young men, saying, "Let her glean even among the sheaves, and do not reproach her."

—Ruth 2:15

Boaz "commanded" the young men. It is surprising how often we have to be commanded to do the right thing! This is especially so when we are called to deal with those who somehow appear to be less than us.

Observe the natural spring of internal resistance, even quiet rage, that springs up within the human heart when we are "commanded." Our resistance to this commanding may not be supported by any rational body of evidence. In fact, had an examination been undertaken, if such was possible, these young men would have been shocked to discover that the only substantial body of evidence condemned themselves! The reapers had earned a bad reputation. That is what Boaz was addressing. Unexamined attitudes toward those apparently less than us should never be allowed to go unchallenged in the Church. Yet they exist just as naturally among us as they did in Boaz's young men. We call it prejudice, a popular word today not always applied well.

The young men clearly were in need of such a command or Boaz would not have issued it. What were the two specific things they were forbidden to do? One was to stop Ruth from gleaning. That is, to say, "You can't get work here unless you are one of us."

Many good organizations designed to protect the worker in the workplace from exploitation become themselves the very instruments of exploitation. They themselves set themselves up to be the best for the situation. They determine the rules that judge themselves, and those who cannot comply, even with a reasonable argument, are excluded. If you're not "one of us" there is no room for you here. This is not the attitude of the Christian Church, even though the Church is an exclusive body spiritually. Even though the Church has standards and conditions of entry that we cannot break, that were commanded by God, whose Church we are. These all being met, we still can fail to be open.

We failed to comply on every account before God, so He Himself made up the difference for us and gave His only Son to fulfill the righteous demands of the law on our behalf so that we could be free from the law and seen as righteous before God and fully adopted into His family. Jesus said, "*Come to me, all you who labor and are heavy laden, and I will give you rest*" (Matthew 11:28). It is an open invitation to anyone to come to Jesus and be received by Him and therefore by the Church. Everyone who exhibits a real regenerating work of God, every one of them, should be welcomed. That's not the Church's rule; that's the Bible's rule; that's God's rule.

We tend to exaggerate the irrelevant issues and minimize the real issues. One way or another, we have a remarkable tendency for getting it all wrong! Boaz had it right. Ruth was allowed to glean, and they must not reproach her.

Reproach is a form of rejection. It sets the individual apart. It lessens them, reduces them. The reproach of Christ is that setting Him "*outside the camp*" (Hebrews 13:13), which He experienced at the hands of His own people, the Jews. It can make the life of the individual seem not worth living. They got the job, they were put in the position, but those who were around them rejected them to the point of breaking their spirit. So there was no need to fire them; they just left themselves! Many a soul has left a church that told them they were glad to see them...so long as they stayed in the pew and did not get too involved! Simply because of an accent or a nationality or a perceived image, superimposed, shaped by prejudice, until that willing, even godly, servant resigned or quietly went away, never to be followed up. Hurting, and finding no comfort.

So Boaz commands and instructs and exhorts over and over. We all need this to be repeated to us often, to counter our natural tribalism and small-mindedness, to say nothing of our lack of practical biblical attitudes toward strangers. He says, "*Let her glean... and do not reproach her.*"

> "*Also let grain from the bundles fall purposely for her; leave it that she may glean, and do not rebuke her.*"
> —Ruth 2:16

Here Boaz commands the deliberate creating of opportunities beyond the instruction of the Scriptures! He tells them to let grain fall purposely. God sometimes expects us to go beyond the limits of our religious codes and to extend love beyond legitimate claims. He "*sends rain on the just and on the unjust*" (Matthew 5:45). Those who are observing this behaviour in Boaz admire him for his kindness. And those who experience such treatment from the Lord are humbled and filled with praise and gratitude for His benevolence.

Note that disobedience in any one of these areas could have so discouraged Ruth that she might have given up and gone back to Moab...back to her gods.

> *So she gleaned in the field until evening, and beat out what she had gleaned, and it was about an ephah of barley.*
> —Ruth 2:17

So we see that while God is going to deliver Ruth and Naomi, Ruth still has to work all day in the field and then beat out the grain. God's deliverances do not necessarily release us from productive labour. Small results from large labour are not to be rejected. God is the Lord of the Harvest.

All this time, Naomi is at home alone, perhaps miserably looking forward to a very small super! But she actually seems to be back on track spiritually.

> *Then she took it up and went into the city, and her mother-in-law saw what she had gleaned. So she brought out and gave to her what she had kept back after she had been satisfied.*
> —Ruth 2:18

So Ruth brought out and gave to Naomi what she had kept back after she had been satisfied at Boaz's meal and, what she had gleaned. The Bible tells us Naomi "*saw*"! This is because it was such a surprising amount of food that seeing it made more of an impression than eating it! This is so often the case with God's provisions. The way He brings His blessings to us, or us to them, is often more miraculous than the actual thing delivered. God's ways are "*past finding out*" (Romans 11:33–36). The meal would be good, but how much better was the surprise at the abundance of God's provision? At this point Naomi knows nothing about Ruth meeting Boaz. This has still to come. God's blessings are endless!

chapter fifty

THE DISCOVERY

And her mother-in-law said to her, "Where have you gleaned today? And where did you work? Blessed be the one who took notice of you." So she told her mother-in-law with whom she had worked, and said, "The man's name with whom I worked today is Boaz."

—Ruth 2:19

One might wonder if this was the first relaxed and ordinary conversation that had happened between Naomi and Ruth since Moab. It has the hallmark of innocent and casual table friendship.

Naomi has blessed Boaz before she hears his name. "*Blessed be the one who took notice of you.*" Her blessing was therefore genuine, not a trite saying. This phrase might easily have become a cultural practice that had long lost any substance. But not for Naomi. She feels gratitude toward whoever helped Ruth.

There should be no reluctance to express gratitude. Never hold back or refuse gratitude. A measured expression is proper, but gratitude at any measure should not be restrained due to things that do not directly relate—the colour of skin, the accent, the social status. The creation of laws to change basic human attitudes is a condemnation against a society. There should be no need for a "law" to enforce such basic things as being friendly. Laws cannot produce a necessary heart attitude, let alone a change in thinking. Only the genuine free expression has real value. When a law is set, it can reduce the genuine, to a mere reluctant, cold obedience. And it can bring the genuine heart expression into disrepute by it being seen wrongly as a cold act of legality.

See Israel passing through to the promised land. Every country that was kind or helpful was remembered and blessed. Those that hindered Israel's progress on their journey were often defeated in battle and plundered. The Bible reminds Israel of these experiences so that they might learn the pain of rejection and the joy of receiving help from strangers. The Lord therefore tells us to remember the stranger. The believer is a stranger in this world, a fact we too often work hard at concealing by our conformity to the world.

Naomi blesses this provider even if he or she does not belong to her little clan or social group. She remembers that Ruth is a foreigner and realizes that any kindness is worthy of note. God of course does nothing haphazard or random, and the helper would provide more than a bag of grain!

> *Then Naomi said to her daughter-in-law, "Blessed be he of the LORD, who has not forsaken His kindness to the living and the dead!" And Naomi said to her, "This man is a relation of ours, one of our close relatives."*
> —Ruth 2:20

Perhaps we should hear a sense of heightened interest in Naomi's voice here. She's recognizing the hand of God. Naomi not only acknowledges the help of Boaz; she also credits Lord. Now this is all indicative of a new revived spirit in Naomi. This recognition of the hand of God in the mundane is a token of a lively spirit in a believer. It can be irritating if extreme, but to see Him in everything is the attitude of the believer walking with God.

Remember, until now Naomi only sees God as having gone out against her. Naomi has been so beaten up by life that she has been unable to think of God and kindness in the same sentence—until now! If only she had kept believing in His affection and love for her, His care and provision. How much of her misery would have been eased, and what glory would have been brought to the Lord, if Naomi had exercised that faith that believes in His goodness? It is admirable when a believer suffers with quiet confidence. It is very doubtful if a "God is against me" attitude is going to impress anybody, God or man.

Naomi also recognizes Boaz to be a relative. Note, she's also saying *"the LORD, who has not forsaken His kindness to the living and the dead!"* Here again we have this ancient understanding of a continuity and connection in a line through history in this family.

> *Ruth the Moabitess said, "He also said to me, 'You shall stay close by my young men until they have finished all my harvest.'"*
> —Ruth 2:21

She tells Naomi about Boaz's instructions. It's wise for a young woman to relay a man's instructions to a more experienced woman, to have her comment on them. Many convincing kindnesses have been turned to curses, and especially for young women. And like most good advice there is a time scale that has to be kept for the benefit to mature, *"until they have finished all my harvest."*

> *And Naomi said to Ruth her daughter-in-law, "It is good, my daughter, that you go out with his young women, and that people do not meet you in any other field."*
> —Ruth 2:22

The warm ratification and guidance given by Naomi here is what we are all looking for from counsellors, family, and friends. Also, where pastoral insights are helpful, we are looking to the Lord to confirm our thoughts or redirect them via clear biblical insights. Naomi says, *"It is good."*

Ruth cannot afford to take any risk. Her situation is vulnerable in the extreme. She's on a sort of probation by Boaz, and by a whole watching society. Naomi expands the situation when she says, *"and that people do not meet you in any other field,"* so that there can be no questions raised about her behaviour. Behaviour is not a private subject! Even private behaviour is not disconnected from the community. What we are and how we shape our lives in private impinges on those around us, whether we want it to or not. The community and its judgments on the individual are relevant. They have to live with us every day. We seem to have lost the distinction between liberty and licence. Liberty is a right; licence is not. "Licences" have to be granted by the community. Naomi is ratifying that Boaz gave good advice to protect the public perception of Ruth.

> *So she stayed close by the young women of Boaz, to glean until the end of barley harvest and wheat harvest; and she dwelt with her mother-in-law.*
> —Ruth 2:23

So was this access to grain some kind of free ticket for Ruth? Not at all! She worked hard right through until the end of two harvests. Boaz is still not overtaken by powerful emotions of pity or pleasure. He will watch for a considerable time before his thoughts are established. Ruth will have to fulfill her commitment to Naomi, and before God, fully.

We have things all the wrong way around too often. The proving of people is necessary. And proving things demands a significant element of time. "*Not a novice,*" says the Scriptures (1 Timothy 3:6).

SECTION XI:
NAOMI IS BACK

chapter fifty-one

BEING PARTNERS

Then Naomi her mother-in-law said to her, "My daughter, shall I not seek security for you, that it may be well with you?"

—Ruth 3:1

Here Naomi says what many a parent has to say to a child. She appeals to Ruth to regard her as a normal mother or even, in this case, a concerned mother-in-law. Naomi wants Ruth to have security. This is what she recommended that Ruth and Orpah seek out in Moab.

Naomi's advice to go back to Moab was thoroughly genuine. However, as we saw, the most genuine and reasonable human advice can be very misguided in the spiritual dimension. "Security" is not worth the cost of turning your back on the Lord God Almighty and replacing Him with a vicious god, made of hand-fashioned cold stone. Today we have enthroned ourselves, wearing the white lab coat of the scientist. The outcome will be no less vicious than with the people of Moab and their false gods. They had the excuse of being somewhat primitive; there's no excuse for those who have a Bible yet act primitive!

Back now in Bethlehem, Judah, it shows the complete circle Naomi has travelled. There may even be an element of apology in it here. Naomi may have been upset by Ruth's statement to her, but it seems no longer the case. *"That it may be well with you"* encompasses the whole of life. We are travelling a journey with Naomi here, a route many need to find, back to a more solid life, to a more balanced existence with the Lord who made us. We need to find Him again as a God who cares, a God all powerful and all good.

In Naomi's mind that was a permanent solution to all of Ruth's problems, permanent in that it would last a lifetime. Now this is interesting in the light of the experience of both of these women! Both of them have the same view of marriage as they did before their husbands died, even though they both died prematurely and though they were left childless! Neither Naomi nor Ruth allowed their own personal difficult times to discolour the enormous benefits of a marriage between one man and one woman. The Bible is still declaring the truth that *"It is not good that man should be alone"* (Genesis 2:18).

So let's step back a little further to get a view of what is going on here that may instruct us, or encourage us, or even condemn us. What's it got to do with Naomi at all? Surely it is all to do with Ruth? Is Naomi just an interfering mother-in-law? Or could it be that there are actually those around us who understand the world better than we do, people who might have a good idea of who would make a good life partner for us? This has not been sufficiently looked at by the present Western world. Not even looked at by the Christian world, yet it is a very common occurrence in this book we call the "Word of God." How many parents, for example, have said, when the marriage collapsed, "Well, we tried to tell them, but they would not listen"? Perhaps it is worth looking at a bit more objectively.

This book is not about marriage as such. This comment is a simple observation of the experience of one young woman. But she is kind of special, is she not? Maybe it's worth allowing her story to influence us a bit, even if not to the full extent. Maybe someone else should tackle the relative merits of such familial influence upon one of life's greatest decisions. As believing parents we are not averse to influencing our children to get a right relationship with God Himself! Perhaps it is our place to influence them also on a life partner?

Naomi's powerful, and quite persuasive, part in this issue here for Ruth seriously affected Ruth, and all for her good. Nobody could suggests other than that Ruth and Boaz were a perfect match! Of course, God was the one who ultimately brought them together. God grant our children such an intervention in their relationships today.

chapter fifty-two

NAOMI IS BACK!

> "Now Boaz, whose young women you were with, is he not our relative? In fact, he is winnowing barley tonight at the threshing floor."
>
> —Ruth 3:2

"Now" indicates a change. Naomi is now a confident speaker! And thoughtful. She is getting her confidence back. What use are our thoughts or plans if God is against us? But perhaps she understands now that He is not against her.

See how the narrative swings from Ruth speaking to Naomi speaking; she calls Boaz "*our relative*," not "my relative." This is not just because he is on Elimelech's side of the family. Naomi now sees herself and Ruth as partners in events. There is no longer any hint of annoyance over Ruth's insistence in coming to Bethlehem. Ruth and Naomi are now a team. They are on to something that could be right!

The beginning of the next sentence is thoughtful and carries an air of possibility. "*In fact*" indicates that Naomi is thinking as she speaks. The fact is that Boaz is a relative. She knows he will be at the winnowing that night because it's her own culture, and she knows the events that take place at that time of year. She had observed them and been a part of them all of her life before Moab. But before we get to the threshing floor, note this: Naomi is back! Old Grumpy has opened her heart to the Lord, the Lord has opened Naomi's heart, and now, in all her beautiful godliness, she's right beside Ruth to help her. Ruth needs Naomi's help.

Winnowing was the last exercise in dealing with the barley. The sheaves were brought onto the threshing floor. This was a slightly raised area of the field, public and open, a circular area twenty-five to forty feet in diameter. The sheaves were placed inside this circle marked with stones. There, they were threshed by a yoke of oxen, which were tied to the threshing machine and walked around the edge of the circle, turning the threshing machine on top of the grain inside the circle. The threshing machine was simply a few boards with nails in them. The nails separated the stalk from the grain on the hard-packed ground, hence the "threshing floor."

After this, the final exercise was called winnowing. Grain and stalk were tossed into the air with a fork, and the evening breeze would blow the stalk away, letting the grain fall back to the threshing floor. The grain would then be stored in a pit or a barn. The winnowing was done in the evening to take advantage of that breeze caused by the warm air of the day rising and the cool air of evening coming in to replace it. So it was dark when they finished, and the heap of grain would be put into storage the next day.[11]

The winnowing is what Boaz did, and Ruth was there too. Boaz then slept at the end, or the edge, of this heap of grain. This was done to deter thieves until it was moved to storage the next day. It was a very public place.

---

11 See Merrill Tenney, *Zondervan Pictorial Bible Dictionary* (Grand Rapids, Michigan: Zondervan, 1967), 227–228.

chapter fifty-three

BEING PREPARED

> *"Therefore wash yourself and anoint yourself, put on your best garment and go down to the threshing floor; but do not make yourself known to the man until he has finished eating and drinking."*
>
> —Ruth 3:3

Naomi's suggestion initially surprises us. This is yet another indication that she is really getting involved in her head and heart about the meeting with Boaz.

Preparation for service always requires "washing" of some sort, physical or spiritually, at times even symbolically. What does this teach us? Washing is a kind of preparation for something fresh. It does remove the dirt of the day, but it removes more than dirt. How many of us have washed away the stress of the day? For the believer, reading God's Word cleanses and resets our hearts and minds to a higher level.

Cleanliness saves us from embarrassment; it gives us a social confidence. It makes us "presentable." It shows the care of preparation, a basic concern for our neighbour at least in terms of initial introductions. For special events we spend much longer to be absolutely certain of our cleanliness. Many a believer spends more time in front of the mirror in the morning than they do before the mirror of God's Word, or in prayer, indicating that we understand the point being made here in the story of Ruth but fail to see its spiritual implications in our lives as believers.

We are a society overly conscious of microscopic germs that might just might—infect us, and only a few of us at that! Yet we seem to care little for glaring spiritual corruptions. These spiritual germs, moral germs, ethical germs, are often more virile that the mere physical germs we are so afraid of.

Being spiritually clean is a common theme in the Bible. In the Old Testament, washing is an external thing, but it indicates an internal purging too. It prepares us for the New Testament washing. "*The blood of Jesus Christ His Son cleanses us from all sin*" (1 John 1:7). Baptism includes the idea of washing along with the idea of death and resurrection. Baptism is an outward sign of an inward experience.

"*And anoint yourself.*" Anointing for the individual was generally with a soothing, relaxing balm or spice. Yet even though it could be a religious rite, it was also for others to sense, the wearers' consciousness of themselves also being heightening.

Even in secular society today, perfumes, scents, and spices all provide a pleasant sense for the wearer but are intended also for the comfort of others. We want to make a pleasant, interesting, and sensible impression on those we meet. Perfumes, anointings, and balms achieve this in most civilized societies in history, and none more so than with ourselves today.

In the realm of spiritual anointing it is an invisible yet sensed "anointing." It is a restrained yet empowering thing. As with simple external perfumes, too much will achieve the reverse of its intention. Here, Ruth's care to anoint herself comes from experienced practice and observation of human responses. God's anointing then, and now, is intended to be invisible, unseen, undeclared, but experienced.

Many of the great denominations of Christendom still employ external anointing to picture the internal anointing of the Holy Spirit. This was an ancient educational tool for the ignorant, but now it is a chain that binds us to the past. Many of these ancient helps have become modern hindrances. They are outdated and perhaps even unbiblical traditions. Many of them are impossible to be discerned by the participant or the observer today. How can we need helps to faith, extra to and other than those prescribed by the Word of God? See how simple the first Lord's table was! See its simplicity become extraordinary when Jesus makes His presence real.

"But do not make yourself known to the man." So when Ruth has washed, with due care, and when Ruth has anointed herself, when she has prepared and is ready, she receives the instruction—to make herself known? No! She is told to remain unknown! Naomi says, *"But do not make yourself known to the man"*! Oh that we might learn this in our crude society. In matters of the heart, we must not be driven by our hearts!

Ruth must listen to instruction that restrains. Of course the degree of heart involvement in this actual event is not at all clear anyway. We cannot superimpose our romantic worldview on to their agricultural, even survival, world view. If we do, we will distort everything out of shape. Ruth is a desperate woman. She's not overly concerned about nice romantic feelings; she needs what Naomi said way back at the gates of Moab—she needs to find rest in the home of her husband.

"Do not make yourself known." Remain hidden, out of sight, not public, not obvious. It suggests humility, even a place of insignificance. This place, when occupied, is the safest place to be before service of any kind. This hiddenness is saturated with a spirituality many never even understand. It is a place God knows well, and He knows everyone He finds there very well. It is a place many servants of God have found down through the ages, a wonderful place for the believer familiar with failings and weaknesses. It is, on the other hand, a thorough irritation to those superficial ones who feel confident in themselves! Only those ignorant of their frailty rush in where angels truly fear to tread.

Jesus so simply infers the importance of this place. He advises his hearers not to take the seat at the top of the table but to wait until they are invited to do so (Luke 14:10). It is the most eternal place on earth. There is no passage of time there. Time seems to have no relevance. It is like a quiet bubble. There is no work there, no striving, no urgency, no dictatorships. No demands. A peaceful restful preparatory "Son bed" where we bask in His delight. God's interest is not in getting things done. His interest is in us knowing His Son, being with Him and happy to be there and not rushing away.

Patient contentment. Peaceful resting. These are the components of this hidden place where we are unknown, but well-known by God. Often we must be forced into this placid timeless valley. Often we must be forced to leave it! We never leave the same as we arrived. We are always changed into His likeness.

So Ruth has a little experience here to teach us about such principles of godliness. If you hunger for such an experience, God will send it in His time. Can you wait? You must! Are you impatient as you read? Seek Him with all your heart. But let Him bring you there. There is no college diploma that grants entry. There is no prayer form that is a key to the place. No retreat, no program or conference, is available. The church you are in, busy or boring, can't provide this experience for you. No other church down the road, no matter what it says or does, can create it. Only God the Holy Spirit can take you to this place of waiting. Only He can make you this unknown yet well-known believer. Indeed, few churches may even be thinking of such a concept. There is only one real book on the subject, the Holy Bible. Read it, prayerfully, and wait on God. He never fails. His timing is always perfect, often surprising, never too late. There is always room for one more hungry soul at His table. You may even be surprised to be invited to sit at the top seat! If that would not surprise you, than it is doubtful that you are the material God is looking for right now. However, later He will bring you to that place, for certain, if you are His!

So Ruth will wait and not make herself known. Her passivity will ensure that she remains unknown. There is of course a time to make yourself known, and Naomi will instruct Ruth about the difference here. We are observing the intertwining of human relationships and God's working with His people. The two have similarities. But the tone is altogether different. Ruth imagines she's doing something at the human level, but she's illustrating for us the principles of New Testament spirituality.

Being Prepared

"*Until he has finished eating and drinking.*" So what is it that will be different after Boaz has eaten and drank? Well, it appears that he will have exhausted his interests for the day. So not only does God want his servant Ruth in a place of rest, He also wants Boaz in a place of rest! But Boaz is not being told to do anything right now. God is working with Ruth. And so Ruth must wait until Boaz comes to the right place naturally before making herself known. Everything has to be in its place before God moves. Then when He moves, everything happens that has to happen, and in its rightful order. It all seems so easy.

Sometimes, due to disobedience or simple human or Christian failure, the one person has to wait an inordinate length of time for the other to comply and fit into God's plan. It's not all mechanistic or ordered beyond alteration. God uses the natural flow to bring people to where He wants them, or to where they need to be for themselves. Boaz will work all day, eat a hungry man's meal, and go to sleep, the sweet, earned, and much needed sleep of "*a laboring man*" (Ecclesiastes 5:12). All quite naturally, unforced, not manipulated. Yet in it all, God is working "*all things…together for good to those who love God, to those who are the called according to His purpose*" (Romans 8:28–30).

chapter fifty-four

THEN AND ONLY THEN

"Then it shall be, when he lies down, that you shall notice the place where he lies; and you shall go in, uncover his feet, and lie down; and he will tell you what you should do."
—Ruth 3:4

"*Then it shall be*": These words are about completion. "Then it shall"! Only when the preparatory things are completed, and in their own time—however inconvenient this may be—only then will things be right. Only then will things combine to fulfill God's purposes. Only then can it be said of the outcome "It shall be"! Here is the sense of heavenly work done. Only then shall it be seen as a special event, a divine event. Otherwise it is a mere extension of human enterprise.

No circumstance can undo the prepared man. God brings him to this place of spiritual rest. Nor can any man ever undo what God does through a life so ready because it is so complete.

"*When he lies down*": When men go to sleep, God still works! This is the experience we want. But we keep getting in the way. Because we keep on working, keep on holding the reins, keep on being in control. Frightened to let go in case... In case of what? In case He fails? Yes! Sadly that is, too often, our secret state of unbelief. So many never see God working!

Wait till the man lies down, says Naomi. Wait until he is exhausted from legitimate effort and not able to function any more; then it is time for God to move His servant Ruth into place. Boaz has no clue all of this is going on! He lies down and, in seconds, sleeps.

Not the thin slumber of the city but the sound sleep of the countryside, hard work, good food, and fresh air.

"That you shall notice the place where he lies": This place of rest, of humble waiting, is not inactive. It is not a vacuum. Ruth is not sleeping! She's alert and listening and here told to watch and take note. This is the experience of those who walk with God. Sitting having coffee, they are alert to the needs around them. They see opportunities that others do not see. They are tuned into what is going on around them, but not in the state of the busybody. Not even in the mood of the spy; they are just spiritually awake. They are waiting for spiritual opportunities. They are expecting them to come, and they are ready to act instantly at His prodding.

Ruth, it's not difficult. Just make sure you see where he lies! We will never see unless we are spiritually attuned to how God works. Ruth goes to the threshing floor with a purpose; we must also go to our place in this world with the same alert sense of divine purpose.

"And you shall go in": Go in! These details are surely to be looked at with some caution, but seriously, what can we learn here? Well, Ruth is now called to action. No longer in the place of resting, no longer a mere follower, as she was on the journey from Moab. No longer waiting, no longer merely a watcher. Not even a busy worker! She must leave the place where she is and "go in."

What is she thinking? She's in a foreign land with foreign customs, and she has no clue other than the advice she has received from Naomi. What an impression Naomi has made on this younger woman! Ruth will follow her guidance to the letter. There is no hint of any doubt in Ruth, no reconsidering of her commitment, no fear.

Naomi must have made a godly impression on this Moabitess. The had known each other for perhaps a decade. Consider those you have known for a number of years. What impression have you left? What trust have you gained? Have you led any to Jesus? Or are you comfortably leaving that to others? What a sad place the Christian church has come to when we often need others to do the most basic Christian thing: speak! We are in danger of becoming people of the "Word" with no words!

Then and Only Then

Ruth is not asked to speak—yet! But when asked she will, without hesitation or fear or excuses or spiritual talk or words to justify silence. Go in, Ruth; the whole of heaven is watching you. The saints to come will revere you. Everyone who hears your name will love you! Like we have already said, obedience is not always difficult. Following God is not all sacrifice, not all chastening, not all heavy cross bearing. Our whole Christian life is *all* obedience. Ruth goes in. What is God telling you to do today? Go and do it!

"*And uncover his feet*": It is so difficult for people today to think pure thoughts. Many have studied the levirate marriage, which is what is thought to be happening here. Let us observe our own private hearts as we read and acknowledge the fouling of our minds. Not by the Word of God! We cannot help ourselves. We read, and before the words actually register on our hearts the actions of Ruth and Boaz are fouled. Yet there is no suggestion that any single thing occurred that was indecent, let alone anything sexual. There is nothing untoward going on here. We must let the Bible speak freely and hold it safe from interpretations that do not reflect the text itself. Let the Bible speak!

Boaz has clearly warned Ruth of the dangers of elicit sexual encounters. He has even protected her from them by warning his young men. He has counselled Ruth to stay close by his young women, all to avoid the scandal of sexual misconduct. Yes, most societies in history would have been scandalized by careless sex! Someone might have died as a result, the woman or the man, sometimes both. In the story of Joseph, every man in a village died because one man let his passions take control![12]

Can you actually imagine a scandal today over two ordinary people having sex outside of marriage? This, however, was a society with a high moral standard. It would be scandalous for Boaz to have a physical relationship here. This society has an agreed position on moral issues. We would do well to follow them. We should read the narrative in this context—the context of a moral society! Ruth has

---

[12] See Genesis 34:25–31, especially verse 25.

also demonstrated a commitment to Naomi and to her God. Nothing wrong or indecent or morally offensive is going to happen. So settle in and see God at work.

"*Uncover his feet*": let's read and understand that as exactly what it says, or as a gentle suggestion to lie close to his feet. It may well indicate the simple fact of Ruth lying there without ever touching him. Boaz was not awakened by any disturbance from Ruth. This suggests that she did not physically touch him. He only awoke when he turned over to get comfortable.

"*And there, a woman was lying at his feet*" (Ruth 3:8): This is not the language or the way of seduction. This is ordinary, plain and simple. All Ruth wants is to get his attention in a very distinct way, a way that conveyed a distinct message to him. It is a very clear and simple declaration, understood instantly by him. There is no innuendo, no undercurrent of any kind. It is the correct cultural way for her to introduce herself on the subject of a very specific type of marriage contract, levirate marriage.

"*And lie down*": And so, the story has moved. It has come from the turmoil of Moab to the tension of a long walk and now to an intense anticipation, here at the threshing floor. Something is about to happening. See again this idea of rest during obedience: "*lie down.*" Just lie down. Sleep if you want, but rest and wait. Here is this calm obedience. Ruth has been doing what she was told to do by Naomi. She's not trying to work anything out or to predict events. She certainly has no intention of intervening or precipitating things. She is passive, and she has no intention of doing God's work for Him, of using her sanctified imagination, of laying her hand upon the ark of God (like Uzzah did in 2 Samuel 6:6–7). She was told to lie down; she is lying down!

"*And he will tell you what you should do*": How good are you at being told what to do, subjecting yourself to authority? Today many church people cannot even begin to imagine the exercise of real authority. Everything is open to debate, and refusal, by everybody else. Authority is a difficult thing to handle properly. The

Then and Only Then

exercise of authority and the obedience it requires in the hearer is a major problem today, particularly in nonconformist churches.

And she said to her, "All that you say to me I will do."
—Ruth 3:5

This is Ruth's response to Naomi. It is good when giving advice to get an immediate affirmation of your advice. Ruth seldom leaves doubt in her answer. She answers fully and freely, giving assurance to Naomi. Here the receiver ministers to the giver. How pleasant it must have been for Naomi to hear Ruth's thorough grasp of and instant agreement to comply with her advice.

Pastors and parents understand this need in the giver for reassurance. The giver is generally the superior in some sense to the receiver, but the giver, in terms of advice or ministry, benefits greatly in their soul when the receiver vocalizes their fellowship in the matter. Ruth gives an assurance to Naomi and thereby ministers peace to her mother-in-law.

By the reading of God's Word we see how He works in the lives of the biblical characters. As we walk by faith we learn to recognize when such circumstances come close to ourselves. Then like Naomi we become people who recognize the hand of God. God's miracles are not all extravagant; nor are they ever trivial. They are always things we could not have achieved ourselves. God's interventions are often, but not always, direct answers to prayer. We too easily forget that true prayer is incomplete without anticipation. Anticipation is an evidence of faith in action. True prayer is also accompanied by an answer! Many of the prayers we have forgotten have been spectacularly answered. Heaven is laughing with bewildered praise at the Lord's amazing answer. But we? Well, we are unbelievably silent! We forgot that we even asked!

Naomi is not a superficial person. Trouble that takes us back to our "Bethlehem," back to the Lord, does not leave us superficial. Difficulties are sent to make us deeper people, hopefully more spiritual, more like the people of God.

SECTION XII: THE THRESHING FLOOR

chapter fifty-five

GOING DOWN

So she went down to the threshing floor and did according to all that her mother-in-law instructed her.
—Ruth 3:6

The conclusion to this passage is given here. Ruth went! Where did she go?

Exactly to where Naomi told her to go, "*down to the threshing floor.*" It is a perfectly normal sentence for the ordinary Jew. Many of the inhabitants of Bethlehem were also going "down to the threshing floor."

We might pass on, but there is something about the language that intrigues. It is what I would call a spiritually perfect sentence! Every word carries the same force. We can read it totally positively, as in a great harvest. The threshing floor work indicated that they had a very good harvest. Or, perhaps more likely for Ruth the sentence could be read negatively, as indicating for Ruth the bottom of a long fall from a happy life down to misery. This is where Ruth is in her spirit. She has been on a "downward" spiral. The loss of a young husband, and no children. Her mother-in-law tells her to go back, then appears to give her silence, at least for a large part of the journey. She leaves her homeland and all that is familiar and secure. She is "down," and here even the symbolism is that she is still "going down"—to the threshing floor.

Back-breaking work beckons her, done by much younger women, done by people probably poorer than she may ever have been. This is being down! She's going down to the threshing floor; that would picture for her and us what she has been through, a divine threshing! And it's called a floor! You can't get any lower than that! Unless of course you are a nameless foreigner as well. The verse gives her no name. "She"! We are probably reading too much and guilty of reading into the text, a common mistake in biblical interpretation. But it's interesting to observe the structure of the language here in this moment.

Of course Ruth is not miserable. But she's human and no doubt has heavy thoughts from time to time during the strain of these days.

This was a very happy evening. She had arrived in Bethlehem, Judah, at the beginning of barley harvest. Now that harvest is at its final night. See Gods' timing in Ruth's life, and expect it in your own in a similar way. At the end of Ruth's misery, God produced a harvest.

It was a happy time. She was in all probability going to the threshing floor that night like everybody else before Nomi spoke to her, although the text in English might seem to suggest it as a second thought. It was to be a celebration. They had more than likely been working all day, so she would freshen up. Washing and anointing were not essentially preparation for seduction! The work of winnowing was not particularly strenuous, not like gleaning, which could be backbreaking in the heat of the day. The evening was a pleasant temperature with a gentle breeze.

The idea of underhanded seductive machinations is stretching every aspect of this story so far. Young or single women did not dress up to impress and walk through the streets of Bethlehem in those days unless they had already lost their reputation! It is doubtful if Ruth was in any kind of party mentality. Life, when it is hard, has a tendency to suppress our lower instincts. Survival is still Ruth's status quo. So she takes Naomi's experienced advice and puts on a "robe"—not her "best" robe as some translations have it. The word "best" is not in the original. There is a strong argument from her widowhood alone that she may only have had one robe! The very robe she wore may have been salt in her wounded life, due to its age and threadbare condition. It was evening, and she would be staying late, and it would get colder. She knew that much. The robe would keep her warm.

So she goes to the threshing floor to winnow. It's just another day in her sad life. She is not beaten in her spirit...I imagine! Nevertheless, see Ruth there, perhaps with a fork or long piece of wood like a paddle, throwing the sheaves up into the evening wind. Or perhaps she did not have to actually winnow, in which case she would still relate to these sheaves being tossed about against their will, even if it did produce a "harvest." Surely she must have observed, during this repetitive action, the wind blowing the chaff away, and the weightier grain falling to the threshing floor. She had been threshed! She had been tossed! Her young life had torn apart. She looked back over a decade or so of trouble that she thought could never end. And looking back, she perhaps realized that the chaff of her life had been blown away, not by mere circumstances but by God's wind of adversity.

She looked back down to the threshing floor, and there, all around her feet, were clusters of pure barley. Something good had come out of the threshing of the barley harvest! Did she recognize among the chaff blowing away in the evening breeze the last remaining husks of her old Moabite life? Silently it had disappeared, perhaps on the winding road from Moab to Bethlehem, Judah. For sure, God, the God of Naomi, the God of Abraham, Isaac, and Jacob, the God who brought her to this very place, would bring some good out of her threshing. Would she see her own personal good harvest?

We know that the harvest she would see was impossible for her to imagine at that point in time. You might be there too! Do not give up! God has a good purpose in store. Rejoice, praise Him, and hide in Him until the trouble passes.

God deals with His children to sanctify them, to remove the excess and irrelevancy from their lives. God is not too concerned about us being "happy." God's interest is in making us something beautiful. Beauty of the godly sort takes time and effort, struggle and trials, temptations, separations, and difficulties. God takes our whole lifetime to work in us to create an image. Not a superficial image like a photograph. Not a surface layer. God's work is a deep work. The image is of Jesus Christ. The old heart has been replaced by a new one. The new heart responds to God.

The Scripture says, *"By reason of breakings they purify themselves"* (Job 41:25 KJV). Breakings, plural! Sanctification is a twofold work: breaking down of the old resistant heart, and then nurturing and feeding and encouraging of the new heart. But the emphasis of this sanctifying work is always on the building up of the new. Sanctification is not eradication; it is counteraction. The threshing floor was Ruth's life till this moment. Now the building-up process begins.

This was the beginning of the barley harvest, a significant time for any agricultural community but more so this harvest for this community. It is called the Shavuot. This was the time of year, in the history of Israel, when the law was given. The law came down to the people at the beginning of barley harvest. And at this time of year, Ruth came to Bethlehem, Judah. As a proselyte from Moab, she illustrates afresh for Judaism the beautiful act of receiving the law of God, as Moses did on the mountain. This is why Judaism holds Ruth in such high regard, such high regard that they read the little book of Ruth at the beginning of the barley harvest every year.

The barley harvest was the first harvest of the Jewish agricultural year. It was a cause for rejoicing, the time when the law of Moses was given, the torah, the ten words, or, perhaps more familiar, the ten commandments. It was also a time for rejoicing and recommitment.

The law had landed in Ruth's heart like it had for them the first time. Though if we remember their failure in waiting for Moses and the incident of the golden calf, it may be that this Moabitess proselyte shamed them by her warm-hearted embracing of God's Law. She goes down to the threshing floor still committed to stay with Naomi no matter what happens.

chapter fifty-six
BEING AN AMBASSADOR

> *So she went down to the threshing floor and did according to all that her mother-in-law instructed her.*
> —Ruth 3:6

Ruth came the threshing floor with intent. The threshing floor was where she would make contact with Boaz. When God works a deep work in a life, He has a specific purpose in mind. When trouble comes in high dosages, it can often be that there is an important event or time coming in your life for which you are being prepared. So here, with Ruth. She has been changed; she's now about to be used.

She's the most unlikely person at the threshing floor to be used by the God of Israel. To those looking on she's a foreigner, easily disregarded. Yet she is God's vehicle for the Hope of Israel down the ages, the Messiah. This foreigner, this Gentile convert, is fulfilling the Lord's will without complaint.

Ruth walks with the carriage of a woman who is God's ambassador. The threshing floor does not have many important people visiting it. This day there were two. Only one was recognized by men. That was Boaz. Ruth goes unnoticed, working and waiting. Ruth will not be distracted. She will not waste her time on anything but Naomi's advice. Boaz, you are in her sights! Oh for such godly, biblical, clear thinking in the Lord's people, in our daily life, church life, private lives, home life—whole life!

A question the Bible raises for us is, How do we view the insignificant person when faced with a problem? God frequently turns our unspoken "class system" on its head. From little Joash in the temple in Chronicles to wee David to insignificant Ruth the Moabitess. All through time. Time and time again. Right up to Jesus Himself: *"Can any good come out of Nazareth?"* (John 1:46). The history of the Christian church has been significantly filled with insignificant people being the significant, chosen vessels of God. So much so that Paul can say, *"You see your calling, brethren, that not many wise...not many mighty...are called. But God has chosen the foolish things of the world to put to shame the wise"* (1 Corinthians 1:26–27). Beware of falling into this trap when the unlikely individual expresses an interest to serve God! Though we must still do the checks and examinations—God does not verify self-ratified calls!

Ruth declares herself with the most humbling, demeaning term she can find. She does not declare herself special. She says, *"I am a foreigner"* (Ruth 2:10). But God is interested only in Ruth down at the threshing floor this night. She is ready to serve.

chapter fifty-seven

BEING EXHAUSTED

And after Boaz had eaten and drunk, and his heart was cheerful, he went to lie down at the end of the heap of grain; and she came softly, uncovered his feet, and lay down.
—Ruth 3:7

So Boaz worked hard all day. He worked with his men as one of them. The work was exhausting, and the more helpers there were, the easier it would be on everybody. So Boaz the noble owner, who stood to make the greatest profit, got down with the workers and sweated his way through the day.

We hear of such examples down the years because they are the exceptions. Many bosses consider it beneath them to work with the men. Many bosses were just plain cruel or lazy. When the individual who is in charge is seen to be working as an equal, his esteem rises among his workforce. Of course, there are exceptions to every rule.

Boaz has exhausted himself working from dawn till dusk. Now he refreshes himself, eating and drinking to replenish his spent energy. This long workday ends in a good meal, It makes his heart cheerful, but no less noble! How many people today think that cheerfulness is found in hard work? Not as many as in other generations. Well, it is actually the meal that produces the cheerfulness, but not without the work! We might do well to hold for a while this simple statement: *"his heart was cheerful."*

Consider when you last sat and enjoyed fun with innocence. An overly busy life cannot find time for cheerfulness. A complaining spirit has no room for cheerfulness. A guilty conscience is too tightly wrung to be cheerful. A contented man can be cheerful. Such was Boaz that night at the threshing floor.

Now we must make it clear at this point that Boaz is not drunk. He is happy. The Bible is not telling us anything other than that he has eaten a hearty meal. He is not intoxicated. He will not have a hangover in the morning. There are things of utmost importance to do in the morning.

Boaz was a noble man. He was a successful businessman. He did not get there, in that society, by being a profligate, a drunk. No, he got there by the diligence and decency we have observed in him in the story so far. His success was due, ultimately, to the blessing of God.

Too many people today want too many parties, too often, for good sense! They imagine partying to be a fundamental, and also a regular, part of life. Not so in most societies in history. There the big event occurred two or three times a year. Not every weekend! And was Boaz less satisfied with life or more satisfied than moderns? Much more satisfied than moderns! We cannot find what we are looking for; we are so twisted out of shape that we cannot find satisfaction! Boaz, now satisfied, cheerfully goes to sleep!

"He went to lie down at the end of the heap of grain": This heap of grain? Could it be to remind us that hard work produces rewards? Or that we sow, but God gives the increase? It might be to tell Ruth that Boaz is able to redeem her. Yes perhaps at the human level any or all of these could be the reason he lay there. The question is, Why does the inspired Word of God tell us this mundane piece of information? Could it be an indication to us, the readers, that our need has already been met before we even mention it to Him? Our God is surrounded by provisions for us.

Here, Boaz is asleep beside an exhausting harvest of grain. And note: it is also a public place!

SECTION XIII:
A STRANGE QUIET WORLD

chapter fifty-eight

BEING QUIET

And after Boaz had eaten and drunk, and his heart was cheerful, he went to lie down at the end of the heap of grain; and she came softly, uncovered his feet, and lay down.
—Ruth 3:7

"*And she came softly*": Now the story takes a step into a quiet, strange world, the dealings of a man and a woman in the night. Yes, this was a unique and accepted cultural practice. A bit strange for us, and sadly difficult for us to view in purity. But this is a pure thing, not in any way designed to do other than what it says. The language is plain to read. She came to where he was lying "*softly*," to be unnoticed, not to seduce. This is an approach designed to do the opposite of seduction, not to disturb the sleeper.

And now we may see why the discussion about relationships took place in the earlier part of the narrative regarding Ruth in the field among the young men! That discourse between Boaz and Ruth and his young men told clearly what kind of man Boaz was. He was a noble, upright man of character, in a very moral society at that. He was not unaware of the problems relating to relationships. He was not naive. He had seen it all in the field at harvest time. Every harvest, year in year out. Harvest by harvest, and no doubt at other times too. But here in the book of Ruth we are to observe an account of the normal but not too common custom of levirate marriage.

"*And lay down*": It is interesting that, at this very tense moment for those of us reading, Naomi is sleeping, Boaz is sleeping, and Ruth is about to sleep. We know the end result. So does heaven.

We, and they, look on as the world becomes silent. Work and activity, thoughts and hopes, all slip into slumber. And for a few solid hours the only movement is God's universe in perfect timing. Nothing changes. No answers are given. No developments that we can discern are going on. Even in the secret places of God that we have no access to, nothing is happening there either! God often works intensely while men sleep—but not here. We nevertheless feel a tension within as we read. How can these three sleep? Answer: because they are tired!

The future of redemption from sin hangs on their compliance! The future of the world is hung in the balance. Can they fail? Of course not! So God can leave them to sleep and order His plans for after they have had a rest from labour. The Lord can give them time to relax and recover from their efforts in the field. They are human. They had earned their rest, and God will let the whole of the watching world, from then until now, just take a back seat while He takes care of his children and *"gives His beloved sleep".* (Psalm 127:2). They will function much better tomorrow, or at midnight as it happens, after some rest.

We find it so difficult to trust. Always remember that in times of need, sleep is still a legitimate and wise thing. God has already provided. The heavenly work is done. There is no rush with God.

chapter fifty-nine

BEING AT MIDNIGHT

> *Now it happened at midnight that the man was startled, and turned himself; and there, a woman was lying at his feet.*
>
> —Ruth 3:8

Is this "*now it happened*" a phrase to introduce a change of narrative, like a literary device? Or is it to be understood as "In the providence of God, at a set time, now," it happened? Surely when it tells us that this happening was at midnight it is telling us that that there was a precise significance about the time it happened and that we should consider this precision. The Word of God is making a point about this very instance. *Now* it happened, not, now it *happened*!

"*At midnight*": Can we see a hint of a suggestion that this day, and all those like it, days of hardship and pain and loss, were ordained to end that night at the stroke of midnight? This was the moment of change or reversal being set in motion, the moment when God declares an end to trouble. And now it happened. Ruth is sleeping, as is Boaz, unaware that God has all but accomplished His work.

"*That the man was startled*": What could startle with such precision? There was no stroke, as such, no bell, at midnight. Not like in modern times when the church steeple bell may ring out the passing of the hours. Surely the invisible work of the Holy Spirit startled the man. Perhaps in answer to Naomi's prayers? One might wonder if, at the silent midnight hour, her pleadings reached the throne of

God. And here in answer to her saintly prayers, God disturbed Boaz. This may well be what startled the man's deep slumber. God, give us prayers that startle sinners out of their deep slumber! One thing is certain: when God moves, He awakens us!

Not all of our prayers reach that throne! Often our prayer are so routine and lifeless that they get nowhere. We hardly listen to them ourselves. Many people who pray every day do not realize that the mere saying of words, religious words even, do not necessarily constitute true prayer. On the other hand, an older widow, as Naomi was—tired, physically, and mentally and spiritually sad after years of burdens, with no energy, speaking with a weak voice and from a desperate heart, filed with faith, believing, knowing her only hope is in God—might well be heard and answered at the stroke of midnight. Note that at the stroke of midnight Naomi would not know this, but we do. Of course God does do things that are not directly related to, or answers to, prayers. Here He is working out His own purposes while men and women are all asleep.

To push the idea a little further, if indeed Naomi was praying, did she sense anything at that moment? Did she keep on praying all night, exhaustedly? Or was she now so close to the Lord that she felt Him calming her spirit to sleep at the same time as He disturbed Boaz out of sleep? God often sends sleep to those whose prayers have been answered. So that as Boaz and Ruth awakened, Naomi returned to the sweet sleep of the beloved. She could because *"He who keeps Israel shall neither slumber nor sleep"* (Psalm 121:4).

"And [Boaz] turned himself": The Bible often tells us that someone turned. The idea of "turning" is presented in the Scriptures when God is about to reveal Himself. See Moses, who *"turned aside"* to see the bush that burned in Exodus 3:4. See John on Patmos, who *"heard behind [him] a loud voice... [and] turned"* (Revelation 1:10–12). It is as though God needs to change the direction we are going in or looking to, even physically, in order to get our attention. Parents say "Look at me when I am speaking to you" to a child they need to communicate with.

Being at Midnight

Sometimes it is because the answer is behind us and we are looking elsewhere for it. Mary Magdalene at the tomb *"turned around and saw Jesus"* (John 20:14). Here Boaz is not looking anywhere. He is asleep, and this turning of himself is presented to us as the first step to a God-appointed conversation with Ruth. One way or another, Boaz turns and discovers not a vision of God but a real woman! His answers are always surprising! Unpredictable, unknown, and unexpected, yet always perfect!

"And there, a woman was lying at his feet": Let's give this a moment's thought. This was at midnight. Anybody would be startled. It was dark. Perhaps not totally dark due to the night sky. It would have been dark enough to confuse a man who just woke up! He recognizes a female form. If a woman was trying to seduce him, he might have guessed that before he even opened his eyes! If she was doing anything unseemly, surely he would have either told her to stop or asked what she was doing?

But note also that the narrative tells us plainly that she was *"lying at his feet."* She was not doing anything other than sleeping. The only reason we go into this is to restrain present day readers from discolouring the passage with this culture's favourite obsession!

Note that the Bible is not afraid of telling us what actually was happening in circumstances of sin. It is not afraid of reality. It requires no sterile code in which to tell us what is happening. The Bible uses ordinary but thoughtful words to clearly show what we need to know. *"Adam knew Eve his wife"* (Genesis 4:1) is a perfectly full description in a perfectly innocent sentence. Observe that here in this story, Boaz did not "know" Ruth! He says to her, *"Who are you?"*

chapter sixty

WHO ARE YOU?

And he said, "Who are you?" So she answered, "I am Ruth, your maidservant. Take your maidservant under your wing, for you are a close relative."

—Ruth 3:9

"*Who are you?*": Boaz's question indicates that the tone of this meeting was pure, with a bit of surprise to wake them up. So no moral outrage is declared. The only thing we have here is a surprised man faced with a situation that needs explaining and is explainable.

"*So she answered, 'I am Ruth'*": This young woman, being demanded to give an explanation, is not embarrassed! She's not a woman caught in an awkward situation. Only a simple question, demanding a simple answer. She will give the answer. But note that there is not any harshness or upset but only a little surprise in Boaz. The answer she gives explains much of the rest!

Unashamedly she states her name. "*I am Ruth.*" Does she realize that he will remember her? We don't know. Humility affects our thinking and how we imagine others will think about us, even if they will think about us at all. Ruth probably spoke with quiet confidence. She is a very determined young woman. Our speech betrays our pride, or in this case Ruth's humble strength.

"*Your maidservant*": When we read that Ruth called herself a "*maidservant,*" this low-class position takes on a beauty that makes her seem like a princess! This is the same humility as when Paul introduces himself as "*Paul, a bondservant of Jesus Christ*"

(Romans 1:1). The humility that is truly godly is not demeaning. Godly humility does not leave us with no self-worth, does not reduce us to insignificance.

Ruth knows who she is, knows what life has done to her, and has come to know the God of Israel, Naomi's God, and understands this renewal. She's not ashamed to stand before this important man. Before she came here tonight to the threshing floor, she stood before God and was accepted in the beloved. Boaz is a mere man. She's a child of God. So, still humble before God and willing to be humble before men, she can speak and make her case clear: "I am...your maidservant."

"*Take your maidservant under your wing*": What does she mean? She's asking him to declare in a practical gesture that he will accept her and protect her and give her security. His wing—this is not in any way suggestive of any human physical contact. It is a picture of the same "hen" that Jesus mentions when He calls to a backslidden Israel and says, "*How often I wanted to gather your children together, as a hen gathers her chicks under her wings, but you were not willing!*" (Matthew 23:37). In an agricultural setting, this is totally descriptive of the care Ruth needs and is asking for. Such phrases are cultural shorthand for much fuller statements. Ruth has a legitimate claim to such care from Boaz.

"*For you are a close relative*": Here the tension of all the midnight confusion is dissipated. Boaz instantly understands the full and only reason that this young woman is lying at his feet. This thrills believers as they see the hand of God on these two people. They deal with each other in circumstances which could rightly be described as dangerous. Yet they deal in such a way that centuries of examination and reading finds no wrong in them. What a testimony to God's work in the heart of sinners!

chapter sixty-one

MY DAUGHTER

Then he said, "Blessed are you of the LORD, my daughter! For you have shown more kindness at the end than at the beginning, in that you did not go after young men, whether poor or rich."

—Ruth 3:10

"*Then he said*": What might we have expected here in such an intense moment between a man and a woman at night? Well, whatever we might have expected, what he says is godly. Let that be an example to all of us when darkness, tiredness, and privacy might make us careless with our words. Boaz, tired as he is, and shaken as he might be by surprise, blesses her in the name of the Lord God of Israel!

"*Blessed are you of the LORD*": His natural response is a spiritual response—he blesses her! He could have told her she was beautiful or wonderful or pleasant, or at the moment he could have quickly responded with innuendo. He could have made no personal comment whatsoever. But he sees God's hand on this meeting, and instantly praise and gratitude rise in his godly heart. It is difficult to knowingly speak evil and at the same time invoke the presence of God. Normally men in sin do not talk about a Holy God. But Boaz has not done anything wrong, and so he is not ashamed to talk about the Almighty. He blesses her in the name of the Lord!

What do we say when someone is kind or considerate to us? "Have a nice day"? Ruth has not mentioned God, has not invited him to bring God into the conversation, but Boaz cannot help himself. He is walking with God. Even when surprised, his response is conditioned by the presence of God. Even when "startled" from a deep sleep, even then, God is on the tip of his tongue. His natural breath is godly. *"Blessed are you of the LORD."* He means, "God is with you, and I am glad!" She looks like a Moabite, not like one of his young women in the field, not like an Israelite. But he accords her the status of those who are blessed by God.

"My daughter!": Boaz exalts the Lord. But he also declares their relationship as pure. He declares her to be his daughter. Figuratively, of course. It may also indicate that she is much younger than him, as is also to be suggested as he speaks on. But nonetheless it is surely a term of moral correctness. Surely it is a relationship of utmost trust and purity. In fact, a relationship that recoils at any sense of impropriety. A relationship naturally pure.

Now it should be noted that Boaz says Ruth has shown him something by her behaviour among his own reapers. Remember, Ruth did not know what field she was in or who Boaz was and certainly did not know his field or his reapers. But she was being watched. We are all always being watched. God said to the devil, *"Have you considered my servant Job?"* (Job 1:8). He invited the devil to look at Job in a variety of circumstances of life, and mostly bad circumstances.

Ruth is not putting on an act at the field among the reapers. She is genuine to the core. We often put on an act for the onlookers, but the onlookers themselves are experienced moral actors, and they see through us. They also recognize the genuine because they wish they were! But they have tried and failed and envy the likes of Ruth. Genuine morality is warm and attractive, even to sinners, for whom it carries a tandem of rebuke and hope—rebuke because they know they should be better, and hope because they see that if the Lord has helped Ruth, He can help them too.

"For you have shown more kindness at the end than at the beginning": Kindness? Where has Ruth been kind? It implies a deliberate action made with understanding about the object of her kindness. But Ruth did not know him earlier when she gained the

good report from the reapers. Here at this time she is actually asking Boaz for a kindness! So how can we explain Boaz's response "*You have shown...kindness*"? It will help us to look at the whole sentence. This kindness Boaz refers to is more than the kindness she showed at the beginning. The "beginning" is when she committed herself to Naomi, giving up her home, country, family, culture, and heathen gods to bind herself to Naomi and her people, her home, and her God and to show that by staying with her for the whole journey to Bethlehem at the beginning of this barley harvest. In this she was doubtlessly contrasted with her sister-in-law Orpah. Orpah gave Naomi a sweet kiss to salve her conscience, then left her to the ravages of life!

Ruth was talked about throughout the whole town of Bethlehem. She was then watched by a whole community and impressed them with her willingness to do hard work and to work beneath her station in life in the barley field behind Boaz's reapers. They saw the way this young woman did what was needed to help her mother-in-law, and they were so impressed as to make her a talking point in their social moments! Well, we can see how Ruth's actions were seen as kindness then. But what is he talking about now?

He is talking about her approach to him. She did not go after the younger men but approached Boaz. He is talking about right now, at his feet, at the threshing floor at midnight. What we have here is not physical excitement but heartfelt gratitude, a subject far removed from our lower appetites. Boaz calls it "kindness." With that thorough wholesomeness the Bible controls elements open to exaggeration and indulgence and keeps them as what they are intended to be, honest and simple acts of kindness. It is not hiding facts or dressing things up. It is not at all sanctifying flaws. The Bible never does this. Here the language is chosen by inspired guidance to keep us from the lies of sinful men for whom purity and simplicity long ago became uninteresting.

Joseph Parker, 1830–1902, is quoted as saying,

Woe to us when we can only live on stimulants! When the house is accounted dull, when only sensational books can be endured, when music and drama and painted show are essential to our happiness, life has gone down to a low ebb and death is at the door.[13]

Boaz compliments Ruth for being kind because she did not just do what many others would have done, then, and now.

"*In that you did not go after young men, whether poor or rich*": Ruth may have been beautiful enough to command a partner younger than herself, it seems. Certainly a partner younger than Boaz. The Bible is wise in not betraying their actual ages. If age had been relevant, it would have been recorded. However, there are unwritten decency laws that should control our behaviour. Believers should show a level of awareness of the character of God and not take advantage of those less powerful than ourselves. God did not abuse His great power. There are endless categories of those who are weaker than us. None are exempt from the care that believers should express for their fellowman.

However, the text here is telling us something about life then and makes a comment that contributes to our understanding now. It may push the boundaries of our cultural conditioning for relationships between male and female, in a healthy way. Boaz is older than Ruth. This was visibly obvious. Boaz said that Ruth's approach to him regarding levirate marriage was a kindness. He did not expect women of her age to be interested in men as old as him, even though he was rich. There were young men who were rich. It would not have been wrong for Ruth to have sought a relationship with any one of these rich young men. Likewise, the whole range of younger men were an open field for her to look at as she was a widow, single, free. Marriage was not about love in the same way as moderns view it. It was about security. That would have been understood as provision,

---

13 Joseph Parker, quoted in *The Preacher's Homiletic Commentary*, vol. 4 (Grand Rapids, Michigan: Baker Book House, 1978), 498–499.

protection, and progeny; children were for the future provision of these securities.

Now the Old Testament speaks of love in all its expressions. The Old Testament societies recognized the heights of pleasure that can be had from certain aspects of love. They also understood that these expressions often have negative aspects if overindulged, both in the individual and in society. Conversely, the love that is about provision, protection, and progeny seldom has negative elements and can equally generate every other aspect of love. They knew that a good set of emotions would do no harm to start with. They knew even better that having children provided a love that lasted beyond the death of a partner. They had experienced the immense worth in a family history, a line of descent, a claim, as Boaz says later, to a place in "the gate" of the city! Children are a gift to a society. They earn us a right to speak at the level of government. After all, our children, whom we have trained in life and society, will take on the burden of the society when this generation is gone. The ancient world was wiser than we are.

Ruth takes the advice of Naomi and makes her initial approach to Boaz. He counts this as a "kindness." His first response is "kindness." What a lovely man! What a sweet couple they will make! But the story of Ruth and Boaz is nothing to do with sweet couples or romance, or getting rich, It's about genealogy. About children. The story is about God providing a redeemer for sinners. God is outworking His own plan made in eternity to redeem men through the work of His own dear Son, the Lord Jesus Christ. This story is about actual relationships that actually produced the generations that brought the Christ Child into the world, often from out of the most amazing and impossible circumstances.

Boaz has no idea of how crucial it is that he marries Ruth and bears children by her. He is still keeping a healthy distance between them. He is not letting the opportunity before him overcome his thinking. He is in control. How often emotional loss of control brings such an emotional high, only to leave us in a mess! Boaz has learned some things in life; he takes control of the situation, insisting upon calling Ruth by the name that will keep them both safe: "*my daughter.*"

chapter sixty-two

MY TOWN

"And now, my daughter, do not fear. I will do for you all that you request, for all the people of my town know that you are a virtuous woman."

—Ruth 3:11

"*And now, my daughter, do not fear. I will do for you all that you request*": Boaz gives his word. Ruth now has something substantial to work with. Boaz has given her something of himself, his word. He also tells her not to be afraid of him not keeping it, perhaps because he himself in his life has been given assurances that never materialized. He has also learned the sheer delight of being a man of your word! Knowing that people trust you with a sense of peace produces a deep sense of self-confidence, not pride. Boaz is a man who keeps his word, and Ruth has nothing to fear.

"*For all the people of my town*": Boaz calls Bethlehem "my town." This may well indicate how significant a person he is in Bethlehem. He is very rich—that we know. But here is a sense of ownership being expressed that goes beyond merely being wealthy. He seems to be significant in Bethlehem. Can you imagine being able to call the place where Jesus would be born "my town"?

What a miracle is the little town of Bethlehem! Rachel's burial place. Young David kept his father's sheep there and was anointed king there by Samuel the Prophet; hence it became known as "The City of David." Jesus was born there, and all its male children under two years old were killed by Herod in his failed attempt to kill the king of the Jews. Interestingly, Justin Martyr (AD 100-165) "said that our Lord's birth took place in a cave close to the village [of Bethlehem]. Over this traditional manger site the emperor Constantine (AD 330) and Helena his mother built the Church of the Nativity...A rich altar is over the supposed site of the Savior's birth. In a part of the cave Jerome, the Latin scholar, spent thirty years translating the Bible into Latin."[14] For centuries, this site has been one of the world's most loved tourist attractions.

Yet, like this book of Ruth, it's just a tiny wee place. What truth the Scriptures declares for us by the prophet Micah 700 years before Christ was born: *"But you, Bethlehem Ephrathah, though you are little among the thousands of Judah, yet out of you shall come forth to Me the One to be Ruler in Israel, whose goings forth are from of old, from everlasting"* (Micah 5:2). Boaz says, this is *"my town."*

"Know that you are a virtuous woman": And it is in this town of Bethlehem that Ruth has a earned a reputation in a very short time. She's known as a "virtuous woman." Virtue is a beautiful characteristic. It is a special kind of righteousness. Its root is in the idea of valour, bravery. It became associated gradually, through time, with the ideal of goodness in all its connotations. Ruth became a widow early in her married life. She could have sought a life of pleasure, but she chose to adopt her mother-in-law, both as a mentor and a guide and as her companion through life. She made that choice decisively. She never looked back. Ruth earned the reputation of being a virtuous woman in life's agonies. Reputations are generally earned in difficulty. The Word of God confirms it, letting it be examined by readers throughout time, and all affirm that Ruth was "a virtuous woman."

Now the book of Ruth is not written as a guide for women. It certainly is a good guide for women, but that would be too restrictive. Here in the wee book before us, we have principles that know no gender barriers. Virtue, faithfulness, commitment, a teachable spirit—these are all present in these few pages of the book. They

---

14 See Merrill Tenney, *Zondervan Pictorial Bible Dictionary*, 111–112, s.v. "Bethlehem."

are all universally honourable and required in all, in all of life, all of the time.

How are we doing today? What reputation has the Christian in the modern world attained? What is the highest standard we have set for ourselves? To be happy people? Irrelevant! To be nice people? Superficial! To be reasonable thinkers? So what? To be virtuous is far above all of these, while not rejecting any of the others.

This virtue is a fruit of faith. A fruit of believing. A fruit of the new birth. Ruth had faith. To Naomi she affirmed, "*Your God [will be] my God*" (Ruth 1:16). Boaz cannot begin a conversation with Ruth without quickly commenting on her virtue. It is something that is "known" about her. The city discussed Ruth and wondered what kind of person she was. When they met her in the field or at the threshing floor or in general commerce, they were impressed. They saw it, they felt it, they understood it, they were amazed by it. By what? By the spirit that exudes from a virtuous person. By her faith in God. The poise and humility that produced. By a wondrous depth and royal carriage.

Ruth was special without any royal lineage. She was chosen by God, called by Him, and she herself did not know it. Unless, of course, deep inside she felt it. Her reputation is awesome and sets her up in the line of the Messiah. Not that she was worthy. Simply that she was chosen.

chapter sixty-three
BEING WILLING TO LET GO

"Now it is true that I am a close relative; however, there is a relative closer than I."

—Ruth 3:12

"*Now it is true that I am a close relative*": Boaz is talking about Ruth's claim to levirate marriage. We understand this statement to mean close in genealogical terms, not emotional terms. Boaz was related to her in family terms through a relative not too distant. Close enough to carry a responsibility toward Elimelech, her dead father-in-law.

The statement by Boaz "*it is true*" must have raised Ruth's spirit instantly. We can feel a sense of excitement rising. Surely this is the answer to all of their needs. Naomi is going to be so happy! But God has more to accomplish than we will ever realize.

In the providence of God things we do not understand are happening all around us that seem strange, even difficult things, yet all furthering God's eternal plan. Many things may be sad or painful. In heaven we will understand it all. We must learn to control our need for complete knowledge. We must clasp every insecurity in the hands of faith and learn to hold it in the suspension of believing faith. And so, just when there is light at the end of the tunnel, just when they have cemented a good relationship with each other, just when God seems to be bringing everything together for good, Ruth and Naomi are about to be thrown into yet another turmoil!

"*However*": Boaz says, yes, I am a close relative, "However"! What a difficult word to hear! Such an immeasurable instant sense of threat! How does a believer respond, react even, to this sort of situation? A situation where everything is again up in the air?

The believer's response must always be hands clasped in prayer! Hands clasped in resignation, not defeat. Disappointment held in suspension is not despair. Ruth is about to be presented with a problem. Will she give up? God is the presenter! Not Boaz. Not ancient Israel. Not even levirate marriage laws. God Himself has determined to set a difficulty in the path of Naomi.

We often see God's hand in our deliverances. Better, to recognize His hand in the difficulties. It takes the cutting edge from problems if we see God in them from the beginning. We are too fond of blaming men when we should see God as responsible—but never to blame! This "however" must have been a shock unforeseen and demanding energy that Ruth and Naomi may have felt they could not muster. But the Bible does not show them in a panic or distraught. Soon in the narrative we will be greatly privileged to be told what they did, how they acted. Their message is still thoroughly accurate and wise. The problem is stated clearly.

"*There is a relative closer than I*": Well, now, should this matter at all? Boaz or another relative? Surely any relative that can redeem? Why the introduction of a relative and why does it seem like a problem when we read it? Because it is a real problem! Partly, because Ruth and Boaz do actually seem to be attracted to one another. If this reading of the narrative is correct, then they have something akin to love at first sight! We can see a suggestion in the earlier dealings between Boaz and Ruth that there just might be something happening emotionally between them. This is hard to dismiss out of hand. Read again his compliments to her. Read again her responses to him. Surely there is at the very least a mutual admiration. Could it be that with the introduction of a nearer relative there also comes a sense of disappointment that Boaz and Ruth might not end up together? Yes, they are both pure and honourable individuals, and in their dealings so far they are to be commended. But we cannot discount altogether that there is a significant emotional attraction there!

Being Willing to Let Go

Ruth does not refuse the intention of Boaz to approach the nearer relative. It's interesting to note the language here. When we read the story from a romantic perspective, the relative described as "nearer" appears farther away than Boaz. Boaz is certainly much nearer emotionally, but Boaz is under threat to be pushed out. Like in many of life's serious moments, the concepts can appear upside down and inside out to those involved.

But there is a more serious issue at stake if we have understood about the promise of the Messiah. He would come through the promised line. Boaz stood in that messianic line. This tender, fragile lineage was often peopled with unexpected men and women. It came dangerously close to being extinguished many times in history. It was forgotten and ignored and shaken and challenged...but God was always in control. This story is one such case where the fundamental promise of God to send a redeemer was threatened.

Yet Boaz does not try to avoid the issue or to manipulate or cheat. He simply sees it as a matter of honesty. A righteous thing to do, even if he would like to have Ruth as his wife. Boaz tells Ruth instantly about the difficulty. Better to get difficulties out in the open before people build up their hopes. How should we deal with difficult matters today? Just the same as Boaz did then, honestly and openly and early in a relationship.

> *"Stay this night, and in the morning it shall be that if he will perform the duty of a close relative for you—good; let him do it. But if he does not want to perform the duty for you, then I will perform the duty for you, as the LORD lives! Lie down until morning."*
>
> —Ruth 3:13

"Stay this night, and in the morning": Boaz is concerned for Ruth's safety. He will not send her out into the middle of the night alone. He will not allow her to walk home through the countryside as a woman alone. Ruth cannot do anything if she's attacked by robbers in the night in a strange land. Boaz is protecting her. He

tells her to stay at the threshing floor. Note, this is a relatively public place. It is not his apartment. The Bible then says nothing more about the night hours. Because there is nothing more to say about them; they will sleep where they are. The narrative then quickly brings us to the mornings events.

"*It shall be that if he will perform the duty of a close relative for you—good; let him do it*": Boaz declares that whatever the outcome of the morning's dealings, they will be "good." Even though we may plausibly assume he is hoping for a particular outcome for himself and Ruth and Naomi, he accepts that the outcome, whatever it is, will be the will of God. This is where his peaceful acceptance of potential loss comes from. He believes in God. He believes in the God of Israel.

Only the believer can reasonably have such a settled spirit about life's disappointments. This is not a mere shrugging of the shoulders and mental discipline accepting the pain of loss. This is the believer's recognition that apparent loss is still the good will of a good God. It is not a bad thing at all; it is not in fact a loss at all. This is the contentment of believing. Boaz can be strong and carry the experience without it reducing him to bitterness about life. The unbeliever cannot be consistent in his anger against a God he says does not exist! His anger is against nothingness. Against emptiness—how is this scientific? He can argue all sort of reasons to modify his disappointments, but he cannot give any real reason for anything if there is no creator, no mind or will behind the universe. He is at the whim of circumstances unplanned, unpredictable, and uncontrollable. This is chaos! This is the atheist's substitute for the intelligent will of an all-knowing, all-good, all-powerful God. Christianity is much more rational that atheism.

"*But if he does not want to perform the duty for you, then I will perform the duty for you, as the LORD lives!*": What a man Boaz is! What a couple Boaz and Ruth will make! They are prepared to let God chose their future for them. He nevertheless gives Ruth the same kind of commitment that Ruth gave to Naomi. He swears by God. "*As the LORD lives!*" As surely as He exists, "*I will perform the duty for you."* He is prepared to act upon the situation of life that God puts him into. He is clear in his mind and fixed in his heart. He is secure in the will of God.

What about Ruth? By this time in the story we have come to expect her quiet resolve to see things through, perhaps with a perceptible expression of faith that expects a good end. Hear the prophet Jeremiah later, but still in Old Testament times: *"For I know the thoughts that I think toward you... to give you a future and a hope"* (Jeremiah 29:11). God wants us to have a life of purpose and fulfillment. In that life, He intends to teach us and change us into the image of His Son. He often even blesses with comforts when we have been in trouble. He promises, *"I...will...restore comforts to him"* (Isaiah 57:18).

"Lie down until morning": Here again we have God letting his children sleep while He does the work.

chapter sixty-four

BEING DISCRETE

So she lay at his feet until morning, and she arose before one could recognize another. Then he said, "Do not let it be known that the woman came to the threshing floor."
—Ruth 3:14

"*So she lay at his feet until morning*": So then, hear it, believe it, and accept it as the accurate account of what happened that night. "She lay at his feet until morning." That's it! Full and complete. The story of that nighttime meeting between Ruth and Boaz is summed up in these few words. It is total innocence, or it would never have been included in the canon of God's Holy Word. Nor would the tiny book have lasted even one generation. The ancients were not shy of detail. They certainly were more subtle in their treatment of relationships than in the present day.

"*And she arose before one could recognize another*": Ruth "arose." Ruth shows a contentment and quiet compliance here. She has done her part, and it has been in secret, from what we can understand. Boaz wants it kept that way, because in his wisdom he understands the public appetite for gossip.

There are sixty-six books in the Bible. and one whole book is given to declaring, to all and sundry, the events that took place this night. Ruth is self-effacing. Ruth does not want a book written about her! She has finished what she had to do. Now she will quietly "hide" herself away through the streets of Bethlehem, away from prying eyes. She goes to Naomi. Only there can Ruth share her incredible story for the moment. She can express all her excitement, her hopes and fears. All the complexity of her feminine emotions can be exposed before Naomi. There will be no judgmental examination. None of the questioning of men that suffocate the loving, faithful heart. She will tell Naomi that she did everything she was told to do.

Not always, but often, in life, finishing something enables us to rise up and move on to the next stage. Finishing suggests accomplishment. It suggests a new stage in development in one way or another. It is so in most areas of life. We break things down into smaller pieces, more manageable or logical, for any number of reasons. Most things fall into natural parts. It is helpful to see life like this in order to get a good grasp of the relationships in one area of life to another.

Ruth had just finished something. She had taken Naomi's advice and done exactly as she was told. It had worked out exactly as predicted. She could now comfortably arise from this and go home to Naomi.

Many believers cannot take this relaxed, settled position with respect to their gifts or callings or mere tasks they have within the body of the church. I have my role; others have theirs. I must do my part. Then I must get out of the way and leave others free to do their part. Many pastors, deacons, elders, even significant members of churches, fail to arise like Ruth did and go home and get out of God's way. They must have some understanding, some insight or oversight, to give or get, even though their actual work is done, even done well. They cannot leave the ark of God to look after itself. We have biblical truth to help us see it from God's perspective! We tend to forget that the church is God's Church, is God's work. We are mere servants. We are not required to "manage" God's work. We are required to be obedient. The Bible does not have a lot to say about us managing God's work; it does say a lot about being obedient to Him as He "manages" fine without us! Ruth does her task and returns home to report to Naomi and receive her next assignment. She does not wait around, interfering.

Being Discrete

This learning of God's ways is a slow and sometimes painful process. It takes a lifetime of practice. It is not the memorizing of a set of rules or verses. Not even learning a whole new set of principles. It is much more simple: the recognizing of His "voice." There are many other voices. But there is always a need for that voice within the believer. The newborn Christian hears it instantly and often. The older often forget what it sounded like. They have stopped listening. It used to thrill; now we don't have time for listening. Take time to listen again. When the believer stops listening to God he often starts listening to his own experience. He often begins to listen to other men's voices and becomes a follower of the latest church fashion.

Books, magazines, websites, conferences, programs, blogs, and so on and so on—our world is a world of information technology. Jesus said, *"My sheep hear My voice...and they follow Me... and no one is able to snatch them out of My Father's hand"* (John 10:27–29). The Church at times seems to have given up the practice of listening to God. And the Bible tells us to learn to listen to Him. But it takes time, and we think we do not have any to spare! Many of us today will reach heaven by the grace of God and the work of Jesus on our behalf, but we will get an awesome shock in heaven. There will be no rush there, and everything will hang on the words of God. There will be no conflicting voices there. When He speaks, all will be silent. And we will be enthralled by the gracious words that proceed out of His mouth.

Some people may not want to go there. It's all about God's ways, all about the divine plan. God sent His Son, Jesus, to die in the sinner's place! No corporate guru could ever have come up with such an amazing plan, and by the way, it produced the greatest, longest lasting, most influential "organization" the world has ever known, and it has no bosses! It does not need them, because it is not an organization at all! In fact, it is an "organism"! It has a life force of its own. The boss, the manager, the organizer is God the Holy Spirit. We are mere servants, one and all!

Ruth was still, at this point just a nobody, despite her virtuous reputation. She did what she was told and then arose and went home quietly. She would not even ask Boaz what he would do now or what timeline was he working on. Nothing but quiet listening and obeying. That's Ruth's example here. Can we learn from her this art of not knowing? The art of waiting, of doing nothing? Being content with godliness? Just happy to sit at the feet of Jesus and worship?

"*Then he said, 'Do not let it be known that the woman came to the threshing floor'*": Here we have Boaz still looking out to preserve both Ruth's virtuous reputation and his own reputation in the community of Bethlehem, Judah. Just exactly who Boaz is speaking to is uncertain. It may have been his servants.

chapter sixty-five

THE GARMENT

And he said, "Bring the garment you are wearing and hold it out." So she held it, and he measured out six measures of barley and put it on her. Then she went into the city.
—Ruth 3:15 ESV

"*Bring the garment you are wearing and hold it out*": How did we get to a simple garment? Here the events of lives and eternity and salvation are being set into place, and the Bible mentions that Ruth was wearing a garment! Oh dear, another difficulty for those who want to distort the text: she is and has been fully clothed all night!

A garment? What's this about? Well, this "garment" is, for one thing, a speechless, silent witness to all that has occurred. It is "on her"; she's wearing it; it is part of her. It is, suddenly and surprisingly, significant. Ruth is set to head off home to Naomi. And into her plan of action God brings a shawl to prominence. She heard a voice saying "*Hold it.*" Ruth could have rushed away. She must have been desperate to relate all of the happenings to Naomi. But she hears and stops to listen again!

Ruth is a good listener. Am I? Are you? She heard a voice. I wonder if she heard another voice in her heart as Boaz spoke. An inner voice. A cautionary, restraining voice. A quiet sense of leading from God the Holy Spirit. Now of course the text is clearly meaning to actually take a grasp of the shawl. It is not telling her to stop! However, that is what it effects. Ruth remains where she is for the moment. Oh that we might be so attuned to that sweet voice of the

Spirit of God that in all our enthusiasm and energy for God we would not lose the grace to stop once more just to hear His voice. The Holy Spirit builds into every believing heart this "voice recognition system." We must culture and developed our spirits until it is instantly recognizable, even when ever so quiet, a still small voice!

"*So she held it*": Ruth is instructed by Boaz to hold this garment. Here is a spiritual moment for those who want to see it. Ruth is here positioning herself to receive a blessing. She held out her garment and then simply held it there in patient confidence and anticipation of the blessing she was sure to receive. This is not a moment of faith but a moment of obedience. Boaz told her to hold out her garment. She did.

Now there is presented to us in these tiny details of this tiny book a sense of poise. A silent, not idle but still brief, moment while Ruth awaits the blessing. She does not rush to fill in this time as though to merely wait was wasteful. Ruth surely understood obedience. To wait is honouring to the giver. Boaz can take as long as he wants to fill the garment with barley. Ruth has no say whatever in this time span.

When God blesses His children, He often calls upon them to wait for what may seem like a long time, yet it may only be a few short days or hours. Sometimes it is a few long years, but wait we must. We cannot go from where we are, and we cannot allow too much distraction beyond the legitimate calls of life and responsibilities. But God seldom arrives too soon. We can argue that He is always on perfect time. This is simply true, no doubt, but it may also ignore the human experience and how difficult we find it to wait, to "hold it."

"*He measured out six measures of barley*": Six measures? God's blessings are measured. They are measured to the maximum you can carry. Surely Ruth could not carry any more than this weight. She was used to hard physical work. No doubt in this agricultural society everybody, even Boaz, even Ruth, had to be able to lift a weight to contribute to bringing in the harvests. Nevertheless,

The Garment

it is a significant weight, probably sixty to eighty pounds, that one might regard as more than enough to carry, even on your back!

When God blesses His children He maximizes it, depending on our ability to cope with the particular blessing. Most times it is much more than we thought we could handle. There are occasions of course when the blessing laid on us is not very much because we are not exercised in carrying burdens for others. It is in carrying someone else's load that we build up our ability to carry spiritual things. God may not be willing to overload you with blessings because you do not overload yourself with helping your neighbour.

Surely Ruth had exercised herself in the carrying of burdens, had she not? She was known already in Bethlehem, Judah, for carrying Naomi's burdens all the way from the country of Moab. Perhaps therefore the Lord knew she could carry this great blessing, big enough for two.

"*And laid it on her*": It was too heavy for Ruth to lift. She could carry it, but Boaz had to lift it and lay it on her. That's God's blessing. He provides the harvest. Ruth, loaded down thus with blessings of barley, makes her way home in the early hours of the morning.

This was before men arose but not the deep, dark hours of the night. Please note however that sometimes God blesses His children in the darkest periods of their life. Then the weight of His blessings, like the counterbalance on scales, eases the weight of their troubles, not necessarily yet undoing their troubles completely, but just a taste of the blessings soon to come—as with Ruth here.

Nobody saw her carrying the great load of blessed barley. This was deliberately timed so as not to endanger Boaz's or Ruth's reputation. But it was also late enough, near dawn, that not many would be around. God knows exactly when to bless us. He knows the world can rob us of His blessing. We must keep it safe until we can share it with God's people first. For Ruth, this would be Naomi, of course. Simply put, charity begins at home! The world will take God's blessing from you and squander it on empty living for self. That's a broad generalization, of course, but as a basic starting point it is sound. It might be that Ruth shared the barley later that day with others, but not before it had been shared with Naomi.

Some burdens should be kept to ourselves, just between the Lord and ourselves, especially those burdens that can only weigh down the free heart. Not every burden shared is a burden halved. Many are doubled! They leave even the seasoned pastor with a heavy heart like your own because there may be nothing he can do. Pray? He does that anyway and does not need to know every detail of your burden to do so. God will fully know what he is talking about!

Often the believer walks alone like Ruth, carrying the greatest blessing the world has ever known, the blessing of salvation in Christ. It is the full and free grace of God expressed in sheer free, unbounded love in the giving of God's dear Son. This love sets us free from the burdens of sin that weigh us down and stifle our lives. The gospel sets us free and fills us with the blessing of the Holy Spirit. We then must walk about this world, sometimes alone in human terms. Never absolutely alone, no matter how we feel. But we carry this burden, a beautiful burden to be shared.

Now this burden will not be halved by the sharing. It will actually be multiplied by sharing. The gospel is to be freely given as it was freely received. Yet often those around us seem uninterested. They are full of things that spoil the appetite of a man for his God. You can be disheartened by this, but make your way to the house of God and there share, in worship and praise to the Almighty God Himself, the giver, and there give back out of the abundance He has given. Learn to know the blessing of reciprocation that abounds in the Christian life at the place of private prayer or public worship, especially at the Lord's table, as the Church gives back in praise to the Lord what He poured out upon them in the few days between Sundays.

Ruth went into the city. She went out empty and came back full! Still, God is not finished yet.

SECTION XIV:
BEING BOAZ

chapter sixty-six

BEING WEIGHED DOWN WITH BLESSING

When she came to her mother-in-law, she said, "Is that you, my daughter?" Then she told her all that the man had done for her.

—Ruth 3:16

"*When she came to her mother-in-law, she said, 'Is that you, my daughter?'*": Naomi calls Ruth "my daughter" again, to show us how close they had become since their arrival at Bethlehem. Naomi is breaking down unhelpful walls by addressing Ruth as "daughter," while Boaz, using the same term with similar affection, is building walls up, to provide a helpful separation.

Words matter! Context matters! Words in this narrative are efficient and safe havens to hide behind. Learn the use of words and their power as a believer. They are the meat of our daily communications, and they are rich and beautiful. They enable us to enrich the lives of those around us. Here in the story of Ruth, good words can separate good people in a healthy way.

See what God does when two people commit themselves to be faithful, to God first and to one another, in difficulties. This, despite differences of age, of race, of culture, but no differences of faith. Two people who share the same belief in the God of the Bible. He pours out blessing that is so heavy that it must be laid on them, blessing that almost overcomes them. We now know that Ruth could not lift but could carry the weight of six measures of barley, possibly around eighty pounds! This is an awesome indication of the goodness of God, even if there is some uncertainty in our understanding of ancient weights and measures. We know for sure that the Scriptures is indicating an abundant harvest for Ruth and Naomi.

"Then she told her all that the man had done for her": Ruth would not have referred to Boaz as "the man" had they gotten any closer than the term "my daughter" indicates! Ruth had not gleaned this barley at the threshing floor. It was a gift, a free gift from Boaz.

> *"These six measures of barley he gave to me, for he said to me, 'You must not go back empty-handed to your mother-in-law.'"*
>
> —Ruth 3:17 ESV

Here we have an interesting comment made by Boaz and quoted by Ruth to her mother-in-law, Naomi. The search for "relational modernity," as we might call it, is fruitless in this story. We are unable to identify any inappropriate behaviour, not even suggestive words, from either Boaz or Ruth. Every action, event, and circumstance is guarded to ensure that no misunderstandings occur. They are pure and do not want to be otherwise.

Even here, the rich, free gift given to the beautiful young woman by Boaz is removed from the danger of being seen as an attempt to buy her heart. It is so worded as to clearly direct it away from Ruth herself to her mother-in-law, Naomi. Boaz removes it from Ruth clearly in case of dangerous connotations. Even a good gift to a poor woman can set a man in danger, and a good gift from a rich man accepted by a poor woman can set the poor woman in danger. Here the Holy Spirit's wisdom is clearly given to Boaz. He is as pure as Naomi and Ruth. They are, all three, pure minds and hearts working together to bring security to one another and to accomplish this safely in the providential working of God! Six measures of barley for *"your mother-in-law."*

chapter sixty-seven
WAITING

Then she said, "Sit still, my daughter, until you know how the matter will turn out; for the man will not rest until he has concluded the matter this day."

—Ruth 3:18

"*Then she said, 'Sit still, my daughter'*": Another moment to "Sit still"! It can be extremely difficult to sit still. God commands us to stay still in numerous forms. To sit, to stand, to wait. He commands this because He is doing something that requires us to stay still and be alert. This command is not the command to rest as in sleep but to pause from activity. To cease from action. To take time to consider, for many reasons, in our walk with God as believers.

God tells the fleeing Israelite nation to "*Stand still, and see the salvation of the LORD*" (Exodus 14:13). There the people of God were to wait and see God do something they could not do themselves. At Pentecost they were to "*wait for the Promise of the Father*" (Acts 1:4). At the ascension they were to watch for the return of Christ in the heavens. Here Ruth is waiting, not to do something or to hear something but to stop doing anything and wait until she "knows" something.

"*Until you know*": Believer, when was the last time the Lord spoke to you thus? Does our life simply move at our discretion? No, not according to Ruth's experience here. Ruth is at the heart of a situation planned in eternity around the salvation of the elect of God. She is crucial to its outworking; she must listen and obey. She has no idea of the enormity of her part in this eternal plan. She cannot be impetuous or lethargic. She cannot just follow her heart, good and pure as it appears to be. She must listen to the voice of God, which right now is coming to her through Naomi and Boaz. She must sit still until she knows something she does not know now, and it is essential knowledge to have before she decides on her next movement.

Sometimes we don't know as much as we think we do. Often we think we know everything when we know nothing. Often what we know is all wrong. Mere intellectual knowledge is insufficient to walk the walk of a believer. Only a listening ear and an obedient heart can enable us to navigate the troubled waters of the Christian life.

How many times have we found ourselves in the wrong place, or in no particular place at all, floundering like a fish out of water, crying out in agony to the Lord, saying "Where are You?" only to hearing an echo of our own cry returning from heaven as the Lord Himself calls to us, "Where are you?!" This because we are not where He told us to wait! Like children, we are! Still we carry on looking when we need to stop! And stay! Until our understanding is filled out to where it needs to be.

Many a man was too impatient to properly prepare for the ministry, so that in ministry he flounders around, learning from a few of the many mistakes he made. And all because his own timetable was a lot shorter than God's. He never yet took time out to sit still, to see how the matter would turn out. His lack of taking time with God may have seriously hindered his ability to function in the service of God, and many such quit, as though the church or God were at fault. Wait "until you know" whatever it is you need to know!

"How the matter will turn out": In Ruth's case it was to observe how a set of moving circumstances would turn out. She had no control over these circumstances. God uses the motions and nuances of nature to further the outworking of His plans. These lifeless mindless forces obey, but man, with all his advantages and privileges, prefers independence, choosing to obey the creature rather than the creator and ending up in many a dead end and many a needless confusion. The believer should be more inclined to be like Ruth and sit still until he or she sees how certain things turn out.

Pausing to consider something ought to be a characteristic of wisdom of the believer in life. Not quick to judge or conclude but patient to wait and let the circumstances answer the questions they give rise to. Taking a long-term view. Not desperate for all the answers today or before the discussion closes. This would make us very strange in a world driven by cellphones' incessant "ticking," like a bomb, which it is, and if it doesn't, we will explode!

chapter sixty-eight
BEING A FINISHER

> *Then she said, "Sit still, my daughter, until you know how the matter will turn out; for the man will not rest until he has concluded the matter this day."*
>
> —Ruth 3:18

"*For the man*": This little phrase, "the man," again gives an insight into the distance that still remains between both Naomi and Ruth and Boaz. Probably less distance exists between Boaz and Ruth due to her working in his fields. But things have moved too quickly for real relationships of understanding to develop. The impression is certainly that there is mutual admiration and appreciation between Boaz and Ruth, and gratitude to God for this from Naomi.

"*Will not rest*": Well, we have made much of resting and waiting on God in the previous pages. But here we have the other side of the coin of human endeavour in the things of God. It may seem totally contradictory to all that has already been said about sitting still and stopping in our tracks to wait. But both are the same message in reverse of each other. The same principles apply to our "moving" in the things of God as to our stopping, our ceasing to move. In terms of our obedience, to do things and get them done. Both require a listening ear and an obedient heart.

The principle is that God is intimately involved in the affairs of our life. He tells us when to go and when to stay. This is not to rob us of self-determination. It is not God's intention that we be robotic but that we be children who listen. It is to keep us safe and allow us to be usable in the things of God. Most days and hours, months and years even, we will come and go as normal but always be thoughtful people. This is because walking with God produces a helpful pace to our life, a pace that allows God to speak to us and helps us to be able to listen. The temptation of the devil is to get us into a frenetic, frazzled state of doing!

When we say this pace allows God to speak, what do we mean? Well, imagine, for a moment, Adam in the Garden of Eden. See Adam there walking and communing with God Himself. It is hard to imagine this as a rushed thirty-five minute business kind of meeting, impossible to see it as a tense, forced thing where if you did not make notes, you would never remember what the meeting was about! Imagine, one day in the Garden of Eden, Adam is walking with God, and Adam is fidgety because the roses need pruning, and the next day God is a bit distracted with the affairs of the universe. So a couple of days later, they must recap, revisit, their hurried lumpy conversation so as to remember what was said.

No, the image of this time together between God and the first man is much more like the time between two friends, companions, on a balmy afternoon with no clock or phone and a perfectly beautiful cultivated garden environment. They never want to leave. They love one another, as God loved His highest creation, "man."

The one word that expresses this talk time is not *information*! Neither is it *organization*. It is certainly not just *conversation*! It is emphatically *fellowship*. You know, we don't have to take notes when we are having fellowship. In fact, notetaking denies fellowship. It keeps our eyes on our page and not on our brother. Imagine Adam with a notebook!

The Lord actually wants our total attention. And we are so engrossed that we do not even hear Him, so much so that we write down the words of the message but miss the messenger. The worship service is spoiled for us because our pen goes dry! Adam did not need to take notes. Neither do we. We like him must "hear" God if we believe that God speaks. And speak He does! At this point in the story, Boaz has heard His voice in full on this matter, and he *"will not rest"*!

Here we have two servants of God, both in obedience to the Lord, who in the same matter are required to do the opposite things. Ruth sits still; Boaz will not rest! They are both taking time to listen for this wonderful voice, the voice of the shepherd of Israel. Both are obedient to act or not to act, as told. Ruth could be impatient, Boaz could be lazy, but both are obedient.

Now here is illustrated for us the capacity required of believers to hear and recognize and understand and obey the Lord's voice in their hearts. This spirit is potently necessary at the meetings of the people of God. When we gather together, we are as one in God's sight. He addresses us as His bride, His Church, His body. We sit isolated by our mind, imagining that God is going to single us out for a special one-on-one meeting. Oh yes, He will, but it will not be when the Church gathers to worship in corporate service. The "one-on-one" talk will be in the privacy of our prayer time.

At neither of these two distinctly different meetings, the church gathered as the body of Christ or the individual in private prayer, will "taking notes" be required. At theological college, you'd better be ready to take notes on your first day. But in the house of God, He wants to look you in the eye. We are so busy writing that we miss a love song! So it sometimes looks like this:

> "Sweetheart, could you repeat that? I didn't get it all. You're speaking faster than I can write."
> "Oh, sorry! I said I l-o-v-e y-o-u."
> "Oh, right, I got it! I will read it later when I have time."

So intense was the listening of Ruth and Boaz in the same situation that they both heard and obeyed what they had to do as individuals. They did the opposite, yet in complete harmony and fellowship with one another and in harmony and fellowship with God.

And so to Boaz, he must be enterprising. Energetic, working diligently, focused and undeterred until the matter he is dealing with has been concluded. He will not let anything hinder him or distract him until he has concluded the matter. He can do it. He will do it.

"*Until he has concluded the matter*": Naomi perhaps knows about this situation in her culture. She judges Boaz rightly. Ruth rests with a sense of hope, waiting quietly for the answer that will surely come.

"*This day*": Well Naomi knows how long it can take to accomplish these transactions. But she knows Boaz will not waste time. He will execute the task given to him and bring it to a swift conclusion.

SECTION XV:
IN THE GATE

chapter sixty-nine

THE FULCRUM

> *Now Boaz went up to the gate and sat down there; and behold, the close relative of whom Boaz had spoken came by. So Boaz said, "Come aside, friend, sit down here." So he came aside and sat down.*
>
> —Ruth 4:1

"*Now Boaz went up to the gate*": And so, as in the early part of the narrative, the family is central. Elimelech and Naomi and their two sons, and then their wives, Ruth and Orpah. The story then goes all wrong and leaves just Naomi and her two daughters-in-law.

Orpah leaves Naomi; Ruth stays. Naomi grasps at being left alone as though she feels some kind of destiny in destitution. Ruth will not leave her. But then, as though making a final statement of acceptance of God's harsh dealings with her, Naomi ceases speaking! She has accepted being alone, but the Lord will not even allow her that choice. So Naomi retreats into grudging defeat, and they stand in Moab, silent. This silence may very likely have continued over the journey to Bethlehem, Judah.

Then Naomi and Ruth reach Bethlehem, Judah, by which time they seem to become a team quite quickly, each recognizing the unique qualities and usefulness of the other. They arrive at the beginning of the barley harvest. Without a waste of time, and due to no earthly plans, this twosome is filling out to a tentative trinity, all in the divine plan of the triune God. Note also a little thing: Ruth went "down" to the threshing floor, where she needs to work. Boaz goes "up" to the gate, where he needs to work. God is with both of them all the time in the same way.

This is where we find chapter 4 of the book of Ruth. The rejoicing over the barley harvest is now in the background. The focus is back to one man, like in the first verse of the first chapter of the book of Ruth when it says *"a certain man"* and takes this one man, Elimelech, and sets him in Moab to die and usher in a catalogue of disaster that's not Elimelech's fault in any direct way. That would be too much to lay at his door entirely. But misery upon misery follow from his journey to Moab. That is the beginning of sorrows in this little book.

Here, at the beginning of chapter 4 of the book of Ruth, we are at another fulcrum of events in the story. Here the balance is threatening to tip against Ruth. Once again it's out of her hands; others will affect her life here in Bethlehem, Judah, like others affected her life in Moab.

One man now stands to determine Ruth's future. And of course by now we know that Ruth's future is bound up with a greater eternal issue she's not aware of, but we are! And so Boaz, alone, goes *"up to the gate,"* as though the Lord is emphasizing His power and not allowing us to think that God needs strength in numbers! Boaz goes alone to the city gate.

This is no mean gesture. Going up to the gate is not an empty cultural practice. This is in fact a very lively act in the community of Bethlehem and surrounds. It's like a council meeting but totally public. It is a place to do business—in particular, business that has a bearing on the community as a whole. So anybody with an interest will stop and listen. Witnesses will not need to be searched for, they will be the community themselves. All of those gathered listen with understanding and interest.

"And sat down there": Boaz sits down. God would have him sit, let him relax, because He will do the work. This will not be a rushed affair. No time limit other than good sense. Imagine, will we, for a moment? They had no watches or cellphones, no written agenda. How could they possibly function? Well, they did for centuries,

and that nation still stands today, functioning to some degree under the Old Testament regulations and guidelines. The society of Boaz's day, the Jews, is still around. So let's not despise "simple" structures.

It is good people that make things go smoothly, not good systems or good technology. There are few things as flimsy and unsubstantial as today's fashions, even business fashions.

Boaz sits down and waits. We do not know how long he sat there, but we do know that he would have waited until the nearer kinsman passed by or was sent for, and he would not move until the matter, as Naomi said, was "*concluded.*"

"*And behold*": Here the Bible tells us, as it frequently does, to "behold"! To stop and look. The event we are to observe is apparently unsurprising—that is, to the reader who is reading the surface facts. It happens as the reader expects. Boaz waits; the relative comes by! But to the trained eye, here is yet another tender link, another fragile thread, in a story far greater than that of Boaz the relative or even Ruth as such. A greater mystery and more serious matter is on hand. The issue here is not finding security for Ruth but the security of the genealogical line of the Messiah, which God has decided to leave to the whim of a relative whose name we are not even given! What if he fulfills the duty!? What if he decides not to be co-operative?

Only Boaz and God are relevant here. God is working, and Boaz is His servant. God has no backup plan, no schemes set in place in case of failure. God cannot fail.

None of the natural threats that materialize can be simply removed by a wave of a wand. The plan of God must survive its trials and difficulties. Even to the impossibilities—it must face even these. It must come through them and not materialize around them.

Here a difficulty is about to be challenged face to face. Boaz is willing to give Ruth up to this rightful relative, if that is what his cultural and religious laws require. And so he sits down, and "*behold.*" We are invited by God's Word to join him for a moment as we read so that we too may behold the awesome working of God.

So many times the work of God in our lives seems to hang by a thread. Fragile it is, tender. But nevertheless it is His work. He never fails. It seems that God would regularly have our lives framed in this kind of fragility so that He can deliver gloriously.

Surely the death of Christ is the greatest such moment, the apparent defeat of God's holy plan of salvation. God's redeemer is killed, by the expert skills of Roman soldiers, who, with all their years of killing, know how to end a life without doubt. Not too much effort, no wastage, a skill learned in life-threatening circumstances on brutal ancient battlegrounds. And there they stand before Him. He is Bloodied, weakened, agonizing, silently. He presents no threat to their skill set. He offers up no resistance to their work. He is like a lamb, Isaiah 53:7 tells us. Not at all like an enemy combatant. Not a fighter by any definition. Without difficulty they kill Him, put Him to death. Their calling in life was this doubtful skill to kill! They made sure it happened. And having watched and checked, with the cold, calculating detachment, they declare Him dead and gamble over His worldly possessions, He who made the worlds and all that is in them. His goods, a single coat, they gamble away among themselves. The matter is now finished. They do not understand, but we do—they have not killed God's plan! They have just fulfilled God's plan!

So here, Boaz seems to have a grasp on the providential power of God. He seems comfortable to take the risk of doing right. Boaz is totally confident in the ability of God to bring Ruth back again, if it is His will. He has heard about Abraham and Isaac. And so Boaz sits down there. And behold, sure enough, *"the close relative of whom Boaz had spoken came by."*

chapter seventy

BEING UNABLE

> *Now Boaz went up to the gate and sat down there; and behold, the close relative of whom Boaz had spoken came by. So Boaz said, "Come aside, friend, sit down here." So he came aside and sat down.*
>
> —Ruth 4:1

"*So Boaz said, 'Come aside, friend'*": "Friend"? The relative had no ill will toward Boaz or Ruth, but nevertheless he could have been seen as a potential threat. Boaz calls him "friend." This tells us something about Boaz. He was wise. Don't judge a matter too quickly. Don't run to conclusions before the matter has played out enough to give a direction or a hint as to its end. "Come aside, friend" is an invitation to something pleasant. The phrase has no stricture or demand. It is a warm invitation.

"*Sit down here*": Posture in a discussion is important. If you want a good outcome, plan a good process. Sitting down is relaxed and removes any suggestion of conflict or threat. It levels people. It suggests fellowship. Having been approached wisely, the preparation, the groundwork of communications, has been set.

"*So he came aside and sat down*": Everything is going well so far, but the issue must be raised. And so the level of the meeting is increased by the gathering of the elders.

> *And he took ten men of the elders of the city, and said, "Sit down here." So they sat down.*
>
> —Ruth 4:2

Here the narrative says he "took" ten men of the elders. This is not forced in any way, but the tone of the language tells us that matters are progressing to the issue.

> *Then he said to the close relative, "Naomi, who has come back from the country of Moab, sold the piece of land which belonged to our brother Elimelech."*
>
> —Ruth 4:3

"Our brother Elimelech" has an affectionate tone. There is no sense here of any recrimination. If there was in the past, it is now past!

The selling of land, in this community, is not a free market profit-and-loss deal like we have today in the Western world. It is an exchange of worth. The land is "bought" for the amount of money it can raise from the next seven years of estimated harvests. So seven years later the buyer will have his money back. And he can return the land to the original owner freely, without loss of revenue, but also without making a profit from his brother. The land is God's land, not ours, in this ancient but biblical view. If any relative wants to buy the land back before the seventh year, there will be a price to make up. The price is arrived at by the years remaining until the seventh year. The buyer must make up the seven years of income for which it was purchased originally. God is involved in this economic system. God is the land owner; we are merely tenants. Land for this community in the book of Ruth is a responsibility, not a bank account. The harvest is ours, but the land remains God's land. And it still is His today.

> *"And I thought to inform you, saying, 'Buy it back in the presence of the inhabitants and the elders of my people. If you will redeem it, redeem it; but if you will not redeem it, then tell me, that I may know; for there is no one but you to redeem it, and I am next after you.'" And he said, "I will redeem it."*
>
> —Ruth 4:4

The narrative explains how Boaz is involved and how the relative is first in line, and without hesitation the relative closes the door on God's plan! "*I will redeem it*"! In this verse the word *redeem* is used five times. It is a powerful word in the Bible. It is a word infused with love and mercy. Redemption is rescuing me from my present owner. It is buying me back and returning me to the rightful owner. Here the discussion is about a piece of land, but redemption in the Bible is a picture of buying back sinners from slavery to sin and death and hell. Here it is a piece of land, but it is about to involve Ruth.

The community all understood the ins and outs of this system. The discussion going on here is mutually understood by all the listeners. One might hope this is the case at Sunday morning worship service in our churches today, that everyone understands all the ins and outs of their redemption by the blood of Christ.

However, the nearer relative instantly says he will buy the piece of land. We might have expected Boaz to be shaken, but there is no evidence of it at all. Ruth and Naomi were not present, but one might imagine they felt it! Yet the believer can actually take such a blow. God never challenges us in things we cannot handle. But God allows this little bump in the road to test them, and often similarly to test us.

> *Then Boaz said, "On the day you buy the field from the hand of Naomi, you must also buy it from Ruth the Moabitess, the wife of the dead, to perpetuate the name of the dead through his inheritance."*
> —Ruth 4:5

Boaz shows the consequences for the relative if he buys back the land. We get the feeling that he knew that the relative would back down, because he does, but that is because we have read the story! Boaz was the type of man who would do the right thing.

This was a business deal Boaz was conducting. It was in full public view and before God. There were witnesses to collaborate this story. Boaz did the right thing instantly, because that was his normal practice in walking with God. This story would have been torn apart by critics through history if Boaz had not told the relative the whole story. Boaz tells the whole story, all the implications and complications. He leaves God to bring about the end, even if it is not going to be the end he hoped for. This is a life of faith we are observing, a walk in daily affairs that is God-conscious.

Boaz seems to have been such a man! He understood that God was in control. What satisfaction must he have felt when the situation that had just spiralled out of his control was handed back to him so easily and instantly. This is a tremendous lesson to grasp and relearn, over and over again. God does not need our schemes or conniving or using people to arrange outcomes. The man of God leaves the outcome to the Lord. He just makes sure he does the right thing and accepts, cheerfully, whatever God does.

> *And the close relative said, "I cannot redeem it for myself, lest I ruin my own inheritance. You redeem my right of redemption for yourself, for I cannot redeem it."*
>
> —Ruth 4:6

This man is continually referred to as the "close relative." He is the obvious choice. He is the one who would be expected to be the redeemer. He has the law on his side. He had custom on his side. He has proximity, "closeness," on his side. The community expects him to be the redeemer. But in all of their expectations they are wrong!

Yes, he looked right, he had all the credentials, and he seemed to be altogether right. But he had one big flaw—he was not able! He did not have the financial ability to redeem the land and Ruth. How true of the religious world. They had it all worked out who would redeem Israel. They knew what he would look like, how he would live and act. They knew what he would do to redeem them and how they would be declared the righteous people of God in the end of the story—but they were so badly wrong!

So wrong were they that they crucified God's redeemer. They put to death Him who came to redeem them! We can be the same.

We think we have everything sorted for the rest of time, but we are often a long way off the mark. How many ideas, schemes, and programs have been delivered to revive the church, to reset the believer on course? But they have failed, and believers are still crowding into the next program to get what the last one failed to deliver. Our focus is all wrong!

Hear what Naomi said to Ruth earlier in the narrative: "*[He] will not rest until he has concluded the matter.*" That is, not until he has "finished" the matter, not until he has "fixed" the matter! Boaz was the right man for the job. He was not a fixer but a finisher! He understood the walk of the believer to do what is right, to finish what he started, but never to determine the outcome. The believer sees himself as a servant and sees the outcome also as a servant.

The "relative" tells Boaz to redeem it all for himself. What a relief is felt here! Though the narrative continues, the work is done.

chapter seventy-one

BEING TENANTS

> *Now this was the custom in former times in Israel concerning redeeming and exchanging, to confirm anything: one man took off his sandal and gave it to the other, and this was a confirmation in Israel.*
>
> —Ruth 4:7

Shoes? Sandals? What are we being told by this?

Well, there are some practical lessons for moderns to grasp. There is a need for some sort of guarantee in deal making, a guarantee that the parties will adhere to the agreement made. Here the agreement was verbal. Imagine buying a property today with only a verbal agreement. Well, for most people in the Western world, the paperwork is only for safety but is never used. This deal may well have been verbal because neither party was intent on cheating or even tempted to cheat. Nevertheless, some sort of basis of trust must be in play.

A sandal? To us this is difficult to grasp as a meaningful gesture, but each party had a matching half! So they could to some degree clearly prove that the deal was made. But underneath the deal was a whole world of cultural implications to restrain cheating. Shoes were not insignificant throwaways! They could be a matter of life and death if you lost one at night in a long, lonely desert walk!

The whole community was welcome to witness the deal. It appears that all those who had an interest in the ownership of property would be there. The community was small enough for everyone to be recognized. The matter was heard in public and agreed in public, and the elders of the community were actively engaged in the matter.

But more than that. There was a clear understanding that God was engaged in the process. How can we be so sure? Because of the understanding that the land being discussed was actually God's land. The field in question was God's field in every sense of their worldview. The buyer and seller were not businessmen like today. They were temporary tenant farmers, working the land belonging for all time to God Himself. So the whole exchange was serious to that community and culture in all its aspects and symbolism. And it worked for generations as effectively as any modern legal agreement between parties on paper!

The believer must have a similar understanding of goods and material possessions. This sense of being a tenant, not an owner, was held by the Old Testament believer. The New Testament believer and the present day child of God must have a similarly clear worldview. We are His children, and He is our Father, and we only have whatever it is we have because of His divine grace. This is particularly applied by us and the Bible to matters concerning our salvation. But it also falls out to our worldly goods.

Everything that concerns us is to be seen by us as a gift from the Lord, held in trust. We are mere custodians. We are servants given instructions by which to order our lives and all that concerns us while here on earth, left to look after things that have their ownership ultimately in the hands of our Master, who is not here at this point in time.

The day will come when He will repossess them, and our engagement with them, the things of this world, will end. The Lord will then wrap them up like a parchment scroll and destroy them as merely temporal tools now redundant. We do not live under Old Testament cultural laws or understandings or practices. But we, like them, live in God's world and have given up everything to follow Jesus. Nothing we have is our own; it is all His. We are mere caretakers.

This view of life will affect our material grasping. It will temper our materialistic internalizing of things with no being at all.

Being Tenants

That material thing that I am clutching to my heart is a temporary and transient event. My investment in it may be very deep and serious—that is, if the thing itself has serious implications for us and or others. But it should never be held so tightly that it affects our walk with God, that step-by-step daily relationship, connection, that balance, that sometimes precarious (from our side) holding together of the two. That present continuous heart engagement between God and me, through the Holy Spirit. That harnessing with Jesus. His easy yoke must not be hampered, twisted, or strangled with temporal things, tripping us, making us stumble away from the path. In essence material things are irrelevancies to the spiritual man in comparison to what life is about for him.

It must be recognized that they have a contradictory ability to hinder the spiritual man in his relationship with God. Essentially, this is a contradictory thing because they are inanimate. Material things have no personality other than what we ourselves have invested them with. They have no soul, no eternal existence. Their only power is in our yielding to temptation. Angels in heaven are amazed, bewildered, by our obsession with rotting, rusting emptiness. *Things* is the word that sums them up. In all of this we are thinking of material things made by men. The world itself, and all that God has given us *"richly...to enjoy"* (1 Timothy 6:17), includes much of what is summed up in this word *things*.

There is nothing inherently wrong with the houses we own or the cars we drive or even the "toys" that amuse and ease our minds. The evil is in us. The corrupting influence is inside us, part of us. We are responsible for the fall of these things, their change from help to hindrance when working against us. The Lord often showers us with blessings of a material sort. He put us into a material world. Much of it is still able to greatly feed the mind, heart, and life of the child of God. Our purposes and practices in serving the Lord are helped and enabled by material things. But even in the church itself, material things can fall into misuse, abuse, and corruption.

In none of these comments are we discussing actual crimes or cheating or changing the use of legitimate things into illegitimate.

We are talking about the walk of the believer, the spiritual man, the outworking of the relationship of the believer with God. Amazing as it may seem to the uninitiated onlooker, the most wholesome religious thing can be turned against us. It only needs to shift ever so imperceptibly from its legitimate subordinate place.

Care is essential in our relationship, in our daily steps, conversations, thoughts, and actions at all time. The believer is a thoughtful person. not overwrought with worry about the challenges but careful and considerate and cognizant of spiritual realities. Hence Paul writes to the Ephesians in a general letter in its relevance to the whole Church, *"Therefore take up the whole armor of God, that you may be able...to stand"* (Ephesians 6:13).

There are subtleties of thought that the believer must handle that when understood will bring peace on the one hand and war on the other. The warfare is victorious only if we understand these spiritual principles.

Where does Boaz fit in this talk? Simply to remind us that in the ordinary affairs of men we must remember, at all times, that we ourselves are morally and spiritually challenged. So are those with whom we deal. A shoe in Boaz's world and culture would be a significant loss to a person. Here the shoe was set as a reminder. It was exchanged not merely to signify that a deal was ratified but as a token of trouble—trouble much more significant than losing a shoe!

The trouble facing the believer in his dealings with material matters are much more significant than the mere losing of one's possessions! We may lose our peace, our sense of His dear presence. Our relationship, as such, may be secure eternally, but chastening may be our temporal lot until we reset our values, reconnect with Jesus, stop chaffing at the bit, and learn to be content in Him, to be thankful, whatever our material experience is at the time. The shoe is about our walk!

> *Therefore the close relative said to Boaz, "Buy it for yourself." So he took off his sandal.*
>
> —Ruth 4:8

This man knows his limits. We do not know even his name. But God often chooses such a servant for such a moment. Elimelech at least was named. This makes me wonder if in heaven all the prominent people in the forefront will be those who were given the background parts in this life. We may not know anyone's name because only the special behind-the-scenes people will be given place! That is probably a myth, but it makes the point.

Back to the close relative: another man may have striven beyond sense to obtain what this man relinquishes instantly. God was not just testing Boaz, Ruth, and Naomi; perhaps He was testing this "close relative" too. They all passed the tests of simple, open honesty and trusting the Lord to handle the outcome. It appears they did so without complaint.

chapter seventy-two
BEING WITNESSES

And Boaz said to the elders and all the people, "You are witnesses this day that I have bought all that was Elimelech's, and all that was Chilion's and Mahlon's, from the hand of Naomi."

—Ruth 4:9

This statement sets the record up to date and straight. It sets the role of witnesses firmly on the public present at the city gate. It lays a responsibility on them to remember this day, to remember this transaction, this event. It briefly but clearly states that Boaz has bought all that was Elimelech's. It is interesting for its clear and firm statement of the facts, so concisely put. But also it is so expressed as to engage the onlooker firmly in the process. They are to be forever witnesses in this matter. This is an aspect of gospel preaching that must never be forgotten.

As the preacher tells of the love of Christ, His suffering death, and resurrection, the onlooker is to be drawn into the event. They must never be left to imagine themselves as mere onlookers. They must understand that they cannot remain passive. Instantly, as the message is preached, they are to understand that their imagined innocence is no longer able to be sustained by them. Now they have heard the good news. Therefore, a response, a movement, is demanded of them by the preacher, by the church as God's witnesses, and indeed by God Himself! This is what Boaz is doing in this business transaction. He is keeping a community alert to essential understandings that might otherwise be lost and disappear.

This may seem far removed from what is expected of preachers today, but it is the time-honoured privilege and responsibility of any believer who speaks the Word, not even just the professional preacher, but the ordinary believer in daily life. We are witnesses. We are called to speak in defence of the gospel and to show its implications and apply them to hearers. This is the character of preaching in all the great preachers through time. It includes the Old Testament prophets. It includes the New Testament apostles. The ordinary New Testament preachers have the same privilege. This understanding is recorded in the preaching of the Church fathers and historic preachers right to our modern day.

Do not lose confidence in God. Be a brave believer. Believe that when you speak you are His ambassador and He will back you up. The Bible tells us that when we are weak, we are strong! Passionate, applicatory preaching is the Church's strength. It is this specific aspect that on occasions raises the anger of the listeners; it touches their consciences. The Holy Spirit owns such applied preaching because it is God honouring. It is not ashamed.

When we worship, we draw people into the experience. We expect people to respond with tears and emotion, raising their hands, even falling on their knees. But when we preach the gospel of saving grace we back off and become apologetic and soft, as though afraid. Perhaps we are afraid? We must not be guilty of emotional blackmail, yet in gospel preaching we should be persuading men, using all means to win some!

Boaz gives an example of a confident declaration in the matter of a mere transaction of land and money. He has a convincing confidence. He makes a clear case, expecting the engagement of the listener.

Of course many a modern preacher is restrained by his congregation or oversight. Let your pastor preach what God has laid on his heart. Do not ever restrict him or silence him. Encourage him to *"preach the word...in season and out of season"* (2 Timothy 4:2). Free him, actively assure him, confirm him in this freedom to speak the Word. If he doesn't speak the Word, pray for him all the more.

But whatever else you do, above all, set him free. Then sit back and sense God's Word freely flowing into your midst.

And finally on this point, understand that all the responsibility to engage and respond positively and actively to that gospel word now applies to you, the believer, in its requirement for faith and obedience. Boaz was an excellent preacher that day, and the witnesses who heard him were so moved and convinced and made certain of their personal attachment to his message that they are still speaking today! The book of Ruth is declaring what happened even as we read. But there was more than just the transfer of land.

chapter seventy-three

THE WIDOW BECOMES A WIFE

"Moreover, Ruth the Moabitess, the widow of Mahlon, I have acquired as my wife, to perpetuate the name of the dead through his inheritance, that the name of the dead may not be cut off from among his brethren and from his position at the gate. You are witnesses this day."

—Ruth 4:10

When Boaz bought the land, he also bought Ruth! "*I have acquired.*" Oh dear, this language conveys more than the sum of its words! Ruth was part of this transaction too. Here this buying of Ruth was seen as something to rejoice in. It was seen by the whole community as a matter for a celebration! Ruth herself appears satisfied with the outcome. Naomi is deeply pleased. The whole community gets engaged. Nobody is upset! Because security is what drives them. Security from starvation. Security against a slow, painful malnutrition. Security against harm physical and mental. Boaz bought Ruth, but he bought her from abject isolation and foreignness, to comfort and security and acceptance at every level.

Ruth gained so much from this transaction that "bought" her that nothing else mattered, especially a word! Can we imagine her complaining? She cannot get over the sheer joy of the vast blessing that has just occurred, expressed by these simple words. What did she gain? Well, Boaz tells us. We should examine ourselves with regards to our priorities as we read the narrative details of the ancients, whose lives carry rich blessings to us all today. Can we learn from them? Yes! If we will!

She gains a husband. This is *"Ruth the Moabitess, the widow of Mahlon."* These two words, *Moabitess* and *widow*, tell us so much about her. Both negative, both permanent. They both declare her poor and vulnerable. She is exactly as Boaz describes her…a foreign widow!

Even right now in our Western society this would be a massive problem for any woman. That is despite our loud declarations that she is "equal." Try telling that to any widow, or telling a widow that she now has an equal "right" to a career path. Don't waste her time unless you are personally offering her a good job! It's so easy to "steal" benefit for ourselves while declaring our concern for another's poor misery. But in truth, it's only a "photo opportunity."!

Ruth had enormous problems, and Boaz solved them. She may still be both a foreigner and a widow, but she is now Boaz's wife! All the status she lacked is now hers, via Boaz. She is now the envy of many nationals, indeed of many married women, because God's blessings have obliterated her problems. This is what gaining a husband did. This is what happened when he "bought" her. This is what God did.

Ruth will have children. All the blessings children represent will excel in her progeny. One of these blessings is grandchildren! And great-grandchildren! And great great-grandchildren! And so it continues. Ask any parent about grandchildren and see their faces light up, even to the bewilderment of their children, who don't quite get it! It is continuity, perpetuation; it means I am not gone when I die. I live on in my children. My name is sustained for another generation.

People take pride in ancient families. If they have remained in one area for generations, they are held in great esteem. They have upheld and supported that community by their effort and commitment, and the present generation is often revered for the work of grandparents. The rampant fragmentation of today, the world over, is not a help to any one of us.

You see evidence of this decay in present-day gravestones being left unattended in modern cemeteries. The stones are worn, the important and unimportant information alike now gone. Unreadable, unrecognizable. Oblivion has reduced them. They have fallen over with the weeds declaring them of no interest, forgotten. Meanwhile the progeny of the previous generations are starting again, in some far distant land, from nothing, to gain a reputation and respect. They lost that foundation with the memories of their loved ones, now gone or long gone, when they left their country of birth. Only a surviving grandmother remembers some details.

We live today not knowing who our grandfather was on one side of the family, or both! Great-grandparents are seen to be mythical figures. Actually, today many a father is a forgotten figure, and that long before he is dead!

"*Ruth... [will] perpetuate the [family] name*": Ruth will have children of her own. What failed to happen in her first marriage will happen in her second. God kept her for this moment. The child she will have will be fundamental to the purposes of God. This child will usher along the coming of God's redeemer, the Messiah, Jesus Christ, God's Son. Much of what God does in the world is unseen. Many of His own people miss His acts in their own lives, let alone on the great world stage.

Many who read the book of Ruth miss the fact that the end of the book is enormously greater than the beginning! The death that reigns in the first chapter is totally superseded in the fourth chapter by the birth of a child to Boaz and Ruth, named Obed. Obed will continue the line of Christ. Obed is a link in the chain through history that would deliver the Messiah. The Christ Child would bring life to the world! We have left off death and famine and tragedy. We are now in events that awake heaven's praise! The angels again will rise as one to praise the God of all creation who sets His way in the heavens, and among men there is no equal.

How often the birth of a child is seen as nothing more. Yet in every child lies an unseen potential. It may take a lifetime to reveal it. In this case it will take more than the lifetime of Obed. It will carry through to the great King David and on and on until one night, when the whole world of men has been exhausted by government taxes and family reunions, a young couple finding no room at the inn will deliver the Christ Child in a manger! Christmas is in heaven's sights when Obed is born. Ruth will have a child as a result of this transaction at the city gate. It was purposed before time began.

chapter seventy-four

THE PLACE OF INFLUENCE

"Moreover, Ruth the Moabitess, the widow of Mahlon, I have acquired as my wife, to perpetuate the name of the dead through his inheritance, that the name of the dead may not be cut off from among his brethren and from his position at the gate. You are witnesses this day."

—Ruth 4:10

Ruth will gain a position *"at the gate."* While Ruth herself would not stand in the gate to speak or debate or do business, she was the catalyst through which the gate was given back to Elimelech. Somebody has to be prepared to be used by God to restore this position in society's "gates." Here in this tiny book we are looking at prophecy from ancient times, fulfilled right now in our own day. Today as you read the Old Testament book of Ruth, you are fulfilling its prophecy as you read. How come?

Well, it says in verse 10, *"that the name of the dead may not be cut off from his position at the gate."* What was this position at the gate? It was the seat that could be taken to discuss affairs of the day by significant families. Business, social, ethical, moral, caring, cultural—any issue of interest or relevance could be discussed communally, the elders being present to adjudicate. Religious issues, and many other detailed and general matters of the society, at Bethlehem, Judah and wider—they all had their place to be discussed, and all at the gate. The gate was the place of influence and where opinions were validated or rejected; where people and practices were examined; where philosophies were stripped to their verbiage and rejected or accepted; where an individual's behaviour, in relation to sexual practices or violence against another or business transactions, commercial or agricultural, could be reviewed before all and judged under the guidance of the elders. Judgments, decisions, rewards, and punishments were all dispensed at the gate. The gate was a profoundly influential place in the life of the city.

Elimelech's place at the gate is being secured and established again, through Boaz and Ruth. These wonderful people see their need to restore Elimelech's place in the gate. He is dead, but his place must be restored. He earned a place in the gate.

God restores us and protects us and looks out for us better than any man or any community. Restoration is a work of God, but it is also a work of the Church. Those who bound Lazarus in grave clothes were commanded to *"loose him, and let him go"* (John 11:44), a command and a privilege often avoided, ignored, or forgotten by the church and its members. Many a believer who was hurt in a church has had to carry that pain every day of their lives and never know what it was for a Boaz to stand up and restore Elimelech's "position in the gate."

This was not merely a statement that Boaz would have children or that a family line would be perpetuated. This was about influence in the society being upheld for the society's good. The blend of opinion, the width of comment, the wisdom available would all be kept full, not left to fall into the hands of a few good, or bad, people. This society valued this truth spoken in Proverbs: *"in the multitude of counselors there is safety"* (Proverbs 11:14). Here it is understood that the more discussion and shared thinking we have in general issues, the more likely it is that we might find a balanced, not necessarily perfect, way forward. These people had a deliberated set of guidelines, even rules, to maintain health in their society. These principles had been established for generations even at this point in Israel's history. To lose them would destroy Israel as it was. The people of God would become just a "people."

This idea is still part of Western civilizations, the right of a citizen to speak on a public platform about matters that concern individuals or society. See the churches use of this public platform to declare the gospel of God to sinners in need of a Saviour, to offer hope to the hopeless, comfort to the sorrowing, help to the needy. See the life-giving stream that reaches poor, sad men and women, orphans and widows, the sick and dying, all at the "gates" of Western society spoken into by God's Church. Its street corners, its market places, its shopping malls, its platforms and parks—all freely available for the society to examine itself with free speech and open debate, where not only free speech is expressed but free, practical help can be dispensed.

chapter seventy-five

BEING BOBBY HAMILTON

His name was Bobby Hamilton. A beat-up Glasgow drunk, his face disfigured by abuse and violence. His spirit had not even survived early childhood, disfigured by poverty and loneliness. Now an alcoholic adult, he staggered to the Barrowland Market. It was at a "gate" in the city of Glasgow, an ancient gate, called the Gallowgate at that time, a poor area of the east end of the city.

The place was teeming with people, just crowds milling about shoulder to shoulder, at times like an angry sea. Pushing and shoving and pressing for a bargain worth a bent penny. Noise and shouting from vendors and public alike. The common smells of alcohol and the poor filling the air. The mass kept you from a chill winter wind. Wee Bobby, as he was, and as he was known, placed his head on his hands on top of a green metal electrical box on the pavement, as the sidewalk is called in Scotland. There he observed the world, his pitiful life written in scars old and new.

Drunk now since Friday night, Sunday afternoon found him in a bit of a state! He could still hear and understand a little. There was a group of people, old and young, standing in a tight circle, playing music and singing joyfully. Bobby swayed to the rhythm. A young fellow told how he gave his life to Jesus and found satisfaction, Bobby shrugged. In his mind he was not young anymore. He looked and felt very old! Yet he was not yet even halfway through his life.

Then a preacher fellow started speaking, an attractive man playing an accordion and with a shock of wavy hair, a man whose likeable presence commanded attention naturally. Bobby was drunk;

he only understood a few words, there in the "gate." He may not even have fully heard the context, but he heard sufficient. The man said, "God loves you."

The world had left Bobby Hamilton a reject, to be ignored and left to die. Pitiless, alone, helplessly bound by the curse of alcohol as his only comfort in the world. Not yet forty years of age, but all forty might have been described by him as "hell on earth"! "God loved him"—really? What a joke!

Bobby rose in his drunken state to object angrily to this assertion by the preacher. How could he be expected to accept such nonsense, "God loves you"? Bobby felt totally and comfortably qualified to challenge, indeed to reject, this out of hand. He demanded that the preacher stop. He shouted, or so he thought, but his mind and voice were both together incapable of making any impression. He did manage to point a shaky finger at this man, who would within a few days become a lifelong personal friend, and say to him in a derisory slur, "What is love?"

Bobby, half falling, half walking, pushed himself into the crowd behind him to make a way from his listening post. He stumbled in a world of his own to his humble little "single" in a dark corner of the city. Love—he had never known it. The phrase irritated him so much that it stayed with him: God loves you! He doubted both concepts, God and love.

In Bobby's day, the motto of the city called Glasgow was "Let Glasgow Flourish by the Preaching of His Word and the Praising of His Name." Bobby had found no help from any father, let alone city fathers. But as he staggered home with an aching heart, that Word through which Glasgow had flourished had landed firmly on his heart: "God loves you." He heard the gospel of Jesus Christ in the "gate," the place where people went to talk and think and act together, where believers went to share the good news to sinners.

But the atheistic city fathers of recent decades thought they did not need God. So they removed the clause and left a void in more than words! Glasgow's abbreviated motto sums up this world's hope: "Let Glasgow Flourish." An empty statement without mention of a way to achievement. Worse, it declares by its reduction that it rejects the only way for any man to flourish! The streetlights that have the full motto embossed on their standards are now lighting a road through a park in Canada.

For the rest of the day, that Word from the gate wrestled with Bobby. It touched him in places no human had reached in his entire life. He fought it and resisted it and swore at it. But as evening passed into nighttime, like the prodigal of Luke 15, Bobby Hamilton came to the end of himself. In sheer desperation he fell on his knees, and leaning on the altar of his worn-out old chair, Bobby presented his scrap of a life to the Lord God Almighty. He had heard "in the gate" that God loved him. He, became a believer that day, called out for mercy and in a moment passed from death into a new life in Jesus. Jesus Christ, God's Son, came into his life and gave him a new heart that was responsive to God. He felt Jesus's love and wept for a long time. He felt a joy, a new energy, and new life within himself. He went to bed but could not sleep.

On Monday morning, Bobby went to his humble, dead-end job and told everyone he had been "saved" at the Gallowgate market open-air meeting. That was Monday. Friday came. Was he changed? You judge.

As was his habit for years on Fridays, straight from work Bobby went to the liquor store. This Friday, like every other Friday, he went to the liquor store and spent all his wages on his usual box of booze. He carried it home eagerly. Silently and alone he set the box on his little kitchen table. One by one, he picked a bottle out of the box. He opened it, with a slick skill. He used to think it made him look cool. Tonight it made him feel peculiarly strong! For the first time in his life he felt like an upright man! Then, to hell's dismay, as he poured each bottle down the sink, he said, in a stone-cold sober voice, "I have the victory over you now," and threw the empty bottle back into the box! Every bottle! Then he fell on his knees and wept tears of gratitude. All from a brief free exchange of words in the gate.

Was this a momentary high? No! Wee Bobby Hamilton never drank again! Never once! He came through cold turkey, as they call it, on his own, in his little room. He required no counselling or drugs or help from medics or men. He just stopped drinking!

But that weekend on Sunday he went eagerly to the Barrowland Market. He waited, for hours, not knowing when it started. The little group arrived. There he went to Raymond Mackeown, the preacher, and told him he had given his life to Jesus. They prayed for him and took him to a meeting that night where he testified about the love of Jesus through tears that had been "bottled" up, unable to be opened, for years.

His story went on like that until he died some forty years later. He never stopped telling of the love of God to sinners. Many of us, younger men, including this writer, had the privilege of travelling around Scotland with Wee Bobby Hamilton, taking meetings and testifying to the grace of God and hearing testimonies of many who heard the gospel of saving grace in that city gate. This all continued for many years until the city fathers decided that there was no room for Christianity at the gate anymore and gradually pushed it out without difficulty. Sadly, with little complaint from the Christian Church.

The gate where he heard the good news was a fountain of life in that free society. But the gate has been given up by the Christian church long before the city shut it down. As individuals and as a body we let it go without a fight. Though our fathers gave their lives to give us a place at that gate, we gave it away without a struggle.

Boaz and his ancient community recognized the danger of losing their influence at the city gate. And Boaz was prepared to give it to the nearest relative, and lose Ruth, to keep the place at the gate, because his interest was in large part to safeguard a place of influence. Note that it was a place of influence for Elimelech, a dead man! Those who contributed to a society by providing children to perpetuate it and serve it and finance it and guide it and fight for it deserve that place to be maintained for their progeny.

This ancient "gate" has been subverted by governments and councils and pressure groups and minorities. Today the gate is a silent unkempt place where lies and fiction rule. Where money talks and truth is silenced—worse, truth is distorted and made to say what we want to hear.

Believers have a rightful place as citizens and as inhabitants of this world to speak. We are spiritually members of another city, the City of God, but while on earth we have a right to speak. So long as governments take our taxes and crave our vote, we have a right to speak in the gate. Finally, and much more important than taxes, whether they will hear or forbear, we have a command to speak as God's ambassadors in His world, wherever we are!

Bobby Hamilton is a modern example of the gate working for society as a whole. They have shut us out of the gate. We need to take it back again. We need to be willing to pay the price to buy our place back in the gate.

The story I have just recounted is from Scotland, my own country of birth. Bobby Hamilton became a friend and a valued contributing member of society as a result of the gate. He became respected and highly appreciated wherever he went. I was in my teens when I met him, soon after he was converted. He left an impression on my young life that has stayed with me until now. He challenged me to live better for Jesus and for men. He was a much better man than I could ever have been.

What I am saying is relative to this concept of having a "place at the gate." Power was given through Ruth for someone who was dead to speak…Elimelech. Now Elimelech represents here the idea of a whole cultural understanding embodied in its citizens that must be heard and not silenced! We too have such a place; we must begin to use it again. It is a priceless right and privilege in a free society.

SECTION XVI: GOD'S PURPOSE BEING FULFILLED

chapter seventy-six
BEING SUPERSTARS

And all the people who were at the gate, and the elders, said, "We are witnesses. The LORD make the woman who is coming to your house like Rachel and Leah, the two who built the house of Israel; and may you prosper in Ephrathah and be famous in Bethlehem."
—Ruth 4:11

The people of Bethlehem, Judah, were witnesses at this gate. Often they were witnesses to their own good judgments being enacted. Often it was a sad day they witnessed. In this passage, none of those present understood the enormous potential that stood before them. An old priest perhaps or a few zealots may have mulled over events in a quiet corner somewhere out of sight. A godly old woman may have felt a stir of more than a romantic or maternal pleasure. Perhaps Naomi was heavy with a sense of divine destiny, not clear enough yet to declare.

What the people did know was that something very satisfying was happening. A wonderful relationship was coming into being, and it was their joy to witness it. They would recount it in years to come over meals in gatherings and conversations. They would feel they were a part of this event. Indeed, they were a part of it! They were witnesses! They declared it themselves at the gate. "*And all the people said…"We are witnesses."* So are we, and to a much greater moment in history, witnesses to the power of the resurrection of Jesus Christ.

They took the joyful liberty of praying over them. They expressed good hopes over the couple. Almost like a priestly blessing they said, *"The LORD make the woman who is coming to your house like Rachel and Leah, the two who built the house of Israel; and may you prosper in Ephrathah and be famous in Bethlehem."*

So here we have that ancient community telling us what they saw as both the purpose and the blessing of marriage: the propagation of a family line; the building of a nation; the provision of care and support for that nation. Rachel and Leah—these two women are given the credit for the creation of the nation of Israel. They "built the house"! It's still here today!

Many family names in Western society are dying out due to lack of children. The really sad thing is that we feel no loss! Those few children whom we have produced to carry our name may not see things the way we do. Sadly, if, or when, they become the oppressed minority in the land their grandfathers built out of wilderness and forest, mountain and lake, they may regret with awful severity their carelessness in the gate. The generations before us did it, without question, to provide for their children. But there are none!

Ruth and Boaz, thankfully, will have a child. The blessing the community conveys on them will be respected, and they will have a child. The people go further and define this blessing a little more for us. They pray for them to *"prosper in Ephrathah"*: the place of fruitfulness. Fruitfulness is clearly a reference to what they have just said. So the people pray that they may prosper in bearing the fruit of the womb—again, and again, the bearing of children.

"And be famous in Bethlehem": the house of bread. Boaz was already well-known for his wealth, and Naomi was well-known for her family history. Yet the people want them to be famous! It's an interesting choice of blessing. Yet however strange, this is their innocent hope. Perhaps it was more of a prophecy than a prayer. If it was a prophecy, even a prophecy of the people, then it was absolutely fulfilled. Ruth and Boaz can clearly be described today as "famous in Bethlehem." Ruth is even in the super-fame category! As are many, many Bible characters, even today! It's a sad world we live in when the super famous are denied a place in our city gates.

chapter seventy-seven

BEING THE DESCENDANTS OF BOAZ AND RUTH

"May your house be like the house of Perez, whom Tamar bore to Judah, because of the offspring which the LORD will give you from this young woman."

—Ruth 4:12

The people at the gate want Ruth and Boaz and their children to be compared to—Who would you have inserted here? Perhaps one of the patriarchs, yes, of course you might. But Tamar and Judah are an odd couple! I discuss this in depth in my previous book *Being Joseph*.

It's a sad tale in every way, apart from its ending. The child Perez is the result of a backslidden moment of desperation for Judah, followed by deceit and cheating and lying. Now, it's a very human story, and we should judge the ancients with caution. However, it is still a sad mark on Tamar and even more so on Judah.

Judah's response to being discovered is interesting. It can be seen to be a truly repentant turning back to the Lord in his life after a period of failure. This is while Joseph was concurrently being lifted up into prominence in Egypt in Potiphar's house. Perez was one of the twins who were the outcome of this relationship between Tamar and Judah.

Yet here, in this spontaneous outburst of happy joy, the people turn—without consultation or planning, even perhaps prophetically—to Perez as an example of blessing and worth! How so? Oh well, we can only play around with thoughts. But it is interesting that God should chose Perez to be the standard of blessing for Ruth and Boaz.

So what is there about Perez that might give us some indication of why they chose him and not, for example, his twin brother? At the birth of Tamar's twins, the first was coming out, and his arm, which was visible enough for the midwife to tie a red cord to, was withdrawn. Instantly Perez pushed past his brother and broke forth into the world, to the midwife's and his mother's great surprise. The midwife said, *"'How did you break through? This breach be upon you!' Therefore his name was called Perez"* (Genesis 38:29). Perez means a "breach," as in a break in a wall. This comment brings together Ruth and Boaz with Judah and Tamar and their offspring Perez and Obed. The emphasis is on the idea contained in the name of *Perez.*

Perez was a breach, a break in a wall. He broke into a lineage that he technically should not have been in! Perez was the unplanned result of a failure in Judah; he should never have happened! Yet in God's amazing providence he is found right in the lineage of Jesus Christ, God's redeemer. What hope for the hopeless! What significance for the insignificant! That's Perez.

The people perhaps see or perhaps simply moved by God's inspiring Spirit account Obed as having made a similar breach. He would be totally legitimate as the child. But Ruth, his mother, is the Moabite foreigner, the Gentile sinner. Although she is now a convert to Israel, she is so recent that she can be still called, still seen as, the castaway heathen and excluded. Yet she has broken in to the family of God! And therefore, by implication, Obed is like Perez, a surprise, an intervention of God into this nation's great future in the Messiah. They expressed it like this: *"Because of the offspring which the LORD will give you."* The rejoicing is all about offspring. The real issue of offspring is only hazily understood by the people. God fills their hearts with joy because He knows what He is doing and spills over some of the joy of fulfillment into their humble believing hearts.

They all stand in the lineage of the Messiah, Jesus Christ. This story of Ruth and Boaz, the story of Judah and Tamar, and all the other stories in the Bible sooner or later return to this theme, the coming of God's Messiah, God's servant, God's Son, to redeem His people back to Himself. The theme is never tiring but always surprising. It is the most glorious theme in all the history of the world and in all eternity. And, despite the interminable problems that attended this plan in the history of the world, heaven will be filled with redeemed sinners from every tribe and nation, in total harmony, around Jesus Christ, our coming King.

chapter seventy-eight

THE LORD GIVES CONCEPTION

> *So Boaz took Ruth and she became his wife; and when he went in to her, the LORD gave her conception, and she bore a son.*
>
> —Ruth 4:13

This is a sweet move to a conclusion in this short story. Yet in our day every believer must give this statement serious and sober consideration, as a matter of urgency. This statement is a significant reason for rejecting the termination of an embryo. The Bible says here, "*The LORD gave her conception.*" Who are we to terminate it? This is what this text in the book of Ruth tells us. God gave Ruth conception; God is the author of life. This is the understanding of the Church in history to this day.

> *Then the women said to Naomi, "Blessed be the LORD, who has not left you this day without a close relative; and may his name be famous in Israel!"*
>
> —Ruth 4:14

These women are anticipating Obed. As in most societies in the history of the world, the women got involved when a baby was born! Most dads in the last few decades have been present at the births of their children too. But in history, the women did what was needed, and it worked pretty well. It's interesting that Joseph was present at the birth of Jesus. But everything was exceptional at the birth of Jesus!

These women declare an advance on the previous *"famous in Bethlehem."* They expand it to *"famous in Israel."* Why? Maybe they thought that being famous only to the extent of Bethlehem was not enough, radical thinking in the restricted worldview of their time, yet fulfilled to the letter! In AD 70, the Romans sacked Jerusalem. The nation Israel was dispersed throughout the then known world, The new Christian church with it. And from there they went to regions that these women could never have imagined. Israel, the Old Testament Israel of God, from faithful Abraham right through to John the Baptist, including the story of Obed, became known. That's fame! But here is also included a whole new world. A whole new branch of the family of believing Israel. A branch grafted on to the True Vine, the faithful believers in Jesus, in the New Testament Church and right until now, to whom Obed is known. Now that is *fame*! God-given fame.

Consider the tiny environment where this was said: Bethlehem, Judah. Consider when it was said: thousands of years ago! Consider what the year is that you are reading in. Consider finally where you are reading this book. Now in all honesty ask yourself, Who but God could have brought this man Boaz, or the anticipated child, Obed, to you in this world at this time, thus fulfilling the prophecy? That alone is a miracle of divine proportions worthy of acknowledgement.

> *"And may he be to you a restorer of life and a nourisher of your old age; for your daughter-in-law, who loves you, who is better to you than seven sons, has borne him."*
> —Ruth 4:15

Here is a hope that parents still have that is often disappointed, to the loss of all concerned—the hope that our children will follow in our footsteps and carry on the message of our life. For the believer, the hope is that our children will carry the flag for Christian truth and practice in their life, and to their children, that we have carried to the best of our ability, and falteringly to be sure. When old age restrains us or we pass on to glory, we hope our children will take up the cross and follow Jesus. Now that would be well described as a restorer of life and a nourisher of old age!

"*Who loves you, who is better to you than seven sons*": In societies or individuals heavily burdened by chauvinism, this is an interesting and wise Word from God. Talking about Ruth, the text says in effect, "a woman who loves you is better than seven sons." They say this no doubt to offer condolences to Naomi regarding the deaths of Mahlon and Chilion. But they say something more full than that narrow application. They exalt women seven times higher than men! Perhaps it was as a corrective balance to chauvinism through the centuries.

Then Naomi took the child and laid him on her bosom, and became a nurse to him.
—Ruth 4:16

This is another old-fashioned practice, continued in many societies even to this day. Grandmother takes the grandchild and nurses him or her. In this case, can you feel the pleasure in Naomi's heart right now? Can you see her smile? Can you feel her heart beat faster? Do you hear her worship and adoration of the mighty God who has brought her to this wonderful moment by His grace? Can you imagine any upset, any discomfort, invading this moment after her years of pain? Not at all! So take comfort and be encouraged! The Lord can do the same for you, no matter your present impossibility.

chapter seventy-nine

OBED BEING THE FATHER OF JESSE, BEING THE FATHER OF DAVID

> *Also the neighbor women gave him a name, saying, "There is a son born to Naomi." And they called his name Obed. He is the father of Jesse, the father of David.*
> —Ruth 4:17

"*A son born to Naomi*"? Surely they meant Ruth? No, they knew what they were saying. See how the Scriptures indulges God's servant Naomi for her years of faithful witness and trust. We have perhaps exaggerated any failings she may have had. The Lord certainly has forgotten them and allows this generous attribution of blessing to her.

Obed means "worshipper"! This tells us what the atmosphere in that community was. It was a day of God's fulfillment of His promises. The whole society was worshipping because Obed was born to Ruth. Actually, it is difficult, well-nigh impossible, to find a distinction in all of this story between Ruth and Naomi. They are totally entwined in everything since their return to Bethlehem, Judah.

Ruth is the central character, we might say, but Naomi is often the star of the narrative. Boaz comes and takes centre stage for a while, but not for long, before he is sidelined at the birth of Obed. But worship characterizes the arrival of Obed because it is a moment of fulfillment. A moment of God's work coming to visual completion to this date. It is, for the ancient people of God, a glorious milestone in their ancient journey.

The following verses are perhaps for the record to show the historical evidence of the movement in God's plan to bring the Messiah to this sad world, just in case we may have forgotten that this story in the book of Ruth is about that plan, is about God! It is about His salvation, right down the ages to this day of grace.

chapter eighty

GOD'S PURPOSE BEING A WEE BOY

Now this is the genealogy of Perez: Perez begot Hezron; Hezron begot Ram, and Ram begot Amminadab; Amminadab begot Nahshon, and Nahshon begot Salmon; Salmon begot Boaz, and Boaz begot Obed; Obed begot Jesse, and Jesse begot David.

—Ruth 4:18–22

Here in this little, this wee tiny book, the book of Ruth, we have a most moving story from ancient times. Their belief in God brought them to this glorious day. Their faith erupted in praise at the outcome of this day. They kept the record carefully. They guarded it with their lives for centuries so that it would not be lost. It is only four or five pages long. So small—how did they manage to keep it safe? "They" could not possibly have kept it safe. God did that, because it is His Word! It is still here. We are reading it, and that alone is sufficient to declare it God's Word.

This closing genealogical list is not a "so the story goes" ending. It is the final declaration of the message of this book, that Christ will come according to the line of David. Great David's greater son. The hope of sinners. He is the only hope mankind has. There is no other hope. There never was, and there never will be. Jesus Christ, whose name cannot even be written in the book of Ruth, whose name is not known to the people in the book, whose coming is so far away at the time of the writing of this little story as to be unimaginable for the characters and the community we are reading of.

Yet it happened, right there in their town! Oh, the miracles of God's work in the world!

The privilege is ours to have seen the fulfillment of prophecy. The birth of Obed takes us eventually to the birth of Christ. We can finish this story properly by reminding each other daily that Jesus came. He died. He rose again. He ascended to heaven. He is coming again!

The Bible tells us, *"The trumpet will sound, and the dead will be raised incorruptible"* (1 Corinthians 15:52). *"And He shall reign forever and ever!"* (Revelation 11:15). The book of Ruth is an essential part of that story. So are you—if you are trusting in the finished work of Christ on the cross for your salvation and have received by faith His gift of new life!

THE END

ABOUT THE AUTHOR

I became a believer when I was thirteen. At seventeen, I felt a clear call to the Christian ministry. It came when I read this verse written by Paul: *"the hearts of the saints have been refreshed by you"* (Philemon 1:7). That notion of refreshing God's people by His Holy Word came to me as a clear call to the Christian ministry. That call and that passion have never left me to this day.

I had so many doubts and fears regarding the awesome responsibility and my own fitness that I didn't go into the ministry until I was forty-four. By that time I had worked for years in the engineering industry, the pharmaceutical industry, and business, where I learned about myself, life, and men as they are. I was concurrently a highly committed member of two wonderful Bible-believing churches. There I learned about the things of God and God's people as they are!

Eventually, and only after the persistent pressure of friends and the Holy Spirit and a further seven years of university, I was ordained a minister of the gospel in a Baptist church in Scotland, where I served for twelve years. I then received a call to a church in Ontario, Canada, where I served for thirteen years. My passion throughout life, and especially during my twenty-five years in pastoral ministry, has been to teach the Scriptures, to "let the Bible speak," and to share the gospel of Jesus Christ at every opportunity. At this point in life I hope to continue in that calling and perhaps, humbly, share the Word of God with a wider audience via writing.

When wee David, faced with Goliath, took up his sling, he said, *"Is there not a cause?"* (1 Samuel 17:29). As I take up my pen, dear reader, I say to you, Are there not still giants hurling insults at God's people? Are God's people not frequently abused, misrepresented, hated without cause, sold into slavery, and alone? Sadly, many members of the family of God have been made to feel solitary by their own brethren, just like Joseph was. Is there not a famine of the Word of God, and have we not become weak for want of it? Then find your Bible again and read it again.

Joseph was equally tried and tested, all by our loving heavenly Father. But by a solitary persistent faithfulness, Joseph prevailed. So may we, by the Word of God.

I have been married to Helen, a nurse, for forty-nine years. We have four adult children and three grandchildren. I have many interests, including old cars, music (acoustic and bass guitar), archery, photography, and watercolour painting. I'm a Scotsman who left Scotland, the "Land of the Bible" (as it was known in better bygone days). I came to Canada, this land of milk and honey, in 2003 to serve a church as interim pastor for six months. God had different plans! The church called me to be their senior pastor, and I accepted. My family joined me in 2004, and we served the Lord there for thirteen years. In 2016 we received the priceless gift of citizenship in Canada. Somewhat ironically, to achieve Canadian citizenship we had to swear allegiance to the queen of England! God has a sense of humour and knows how to keep a Scotsman humble!

Also by the Author

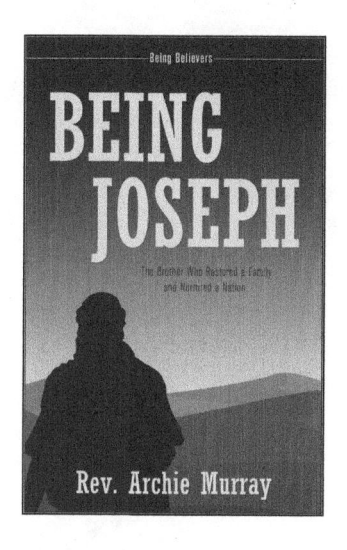

Being Joseph
ISBN:978–1–4866–1573–5

Have you ever felt betrayed by a family member? Have you ever needed even a glimpse of hope to help you through a tough situation? In the Old Testament, we read that Joseph was thrown into a pit and then sold by his own brothers. This great betrayal left him feeling alone and in despair. Unfortunately, this was only the beginning of his troubles.

Being Joseph takes a closer, pastoral perspective on perseverance through hardships, the value of forgiveness even when it's near impossible, and the redemptive hope of reconciliation. Joseph's story expands on dreams, slavery, seduction, imprisonment, and the restoration of a family. In the worst moments of Joseph's life, we can see that God never left his side. The lessons we can learn from this book can help enrich our daily lives in this difficult world today.

All ages will benefit from this captivating commentary on a real family, just like yours.

Watch for the next instalment, *Being Joshua*, coming soon!